ΑΝΑΓΚΗ IN THUCYDIDES

American Philological Association
American Classical Studies

The Harmonics of Nicomachus and the Pythagorean Tradition	Flora R. Levin
The Etymology and the Usage of ΠΕΙΡΑΡ in Early Greek Poetry	Ann L. T. Bergren
Two Studies in Roman Nomenclature	D.R. Shackleton Bailey
The Latin Particle Quidem	J. Solodow
On the Hymn to Zeus in Aeschylus' Agamemnon	Peter M. Smith
The Andromache of Euripides	Paul David Kovacs
A Commentary on the Vita Hadriani in the Historia Augusta	Herbert W. Benario
Creation and Salvation in Ancient Orphism	Larry J. Alderink
Eros Sophistes: Ancient Novelists at Play	Graham Anderson
Ancient Philosophy and Grammar: The Syntax of Apollonius Dyscolus	David Blank
Autonomia: Its Genesis and Early History	Martin Ostwald
Language and Metre: Resolution, Porson's Bridge, and Their Prosodic Basis	A. M. Devine
Descent from Heaven: Images of Dew in Greek Poetry and Religion	Deborah Boedeker
Iamblichus and the Theory of the Vehicle of the Soul	John F. Finamore
Epicurus on the Swerve and Voluntary Action	Walter G. Englert
Seneca's Anapaests	John G. Fitch
<u>Xoana</u> *and the Origins of Greek Sculpture*	A. A. Donohue
ΑΝΑΓΚΗ in Thucydides	Martin Ostwald

Martin Ostwald

ΑΝΑΓΚΗ IN THUCYDIDES

Scholars Press
Atlanta, Georgia

ΑΝΑΓΚΗ IN THUCYDIDES

Martin Ostwald

© 1988
The American Philological Association

Library of Congress Cataloging in Publication Data
Ostwald, Martin, 1922-
  Ananke in Thucydides.

  (American classical studies ;)
  "An expanded version of a presidential address delivered before the annual meeting of the American Philological Association in New York on December 29, 1987"--Pref.
  Bibliography: p.
  Includes index.
  1. Thucydides. History of the Peloponnesian War.
2. Greece--History--Peloponnesian War, 431-404 B.C.--Historiography. 3. Ananke (The Greek Word) I. Title.
II. Series.
DF229.T6077   1989   938'.05   88-32781
ISBN: 978-1-55540-280-8

ΑΝΑΓΚΗ in Thucydides

	Preface	VII
I.	The Problem of Thucydides I.23.6	1
II.	The Connotations of Ἀνάγκη in Thucydides	7
III.	Historical Method and the Outbreak of the Peloponnesian War	21
IV.	Ἀνάγκη and the History of the Peloponnesian War	33
V.	Ἀνάγκη and Morality	53
VI.	Conclusion: The Use of History	63
	Indices	
	Bibliography	67
	Index Locorum	73
	Greek Index	77
	General Index	79

Preface

This monograph is an expanded version of a presidential address delivered before the annual meeting of the American Philological Association in New York on December 29, 1987. It was composed during a leave from my teaching duties at Swarthmore College and the University of Pennsylvania in 1986-87. For making that leave possible, I wish to express my gratitude not only to these two institutions but particularly to Swarthmore College for the award of a Eugene M. Lang Faculty Fellowship and to Mr. Eugene M. Lang for generously endowing this fellowship fund.

For providing a most pleasant and congenial atmosphere for my research and writing and for generous hospitality extended to my wife and myself, I owe cordial thanks to the American Academy in Rome and its administration and staff, and to Wolfson College, Oxford, and its President and Fellows who honored me with the award of a Visting Fellowship.

Many friends have improved this monograph through their criticism. Without the keen eyes of Stewart Flory, Helen North, A. John Graham, Ludwig Koenen, and two anonymous readers for the Monograph Series of the American Philological Association it would contain more flawed arguments and errors of judgment than are still left in it. For improvements of style I am indebted to Sarah Fought. I assure them all of my deep appreciation for their help and absolve them of any responsibility for the imperfections that remain. To the editorial board of the Monograph Series of the American Philological Association I am grateful for accepting this work for publication.

Swarthmore College
and University of Pennsylvania
May 1988   M.O.

Ch. I. The Problem of Thucydides I.23.6

It is difficult to think of any single passage in ancient Greek literature that has given rise to more intense controversy than Thucydides' statement on the causes of the Peloponnesian War: τὴν μὲν γὰρ ἀληθεστάτην πρόφασιν, ἀφανεστάτην δὲ λόγῳ, τοὺς Ἀθηναίους ἡγοῦμαι μεγάλους γιγνομένους καὶ φόβον παρέχοντας τοῖς Λακεδαιμονίοις ἀναγκάσαι ἐς τὸ πολεμεῖν· αἱ δ' ἐς τὸ φανερὸν λεγόμεναι αἰτίαι αἵδ' ἦσαν ἑκατέρων, ἀφ' ὧν λύσαντες τὰς σπονδὰς ἐς τὸν πόλεμον κατέστησαν.[1] The accuracy of the transmitted text has, to the best of my knowledge, never been in serious doubt. But much ink has been spilled over the precise connotation of πρόφασις in this context and its distinction from αἰτίαι,[2] and in its train over the question whether Athens or Sparta bears the greater blame for the outbreak of hostilities. Despite the controversy, however, the distinction Thucydides posits between a deeper and more immediate causes remains intelligible: αἰτίαι, characterized as "openly alleged" (ἐς τὸ φανερὸν λεγόμεναι), obviously include the charges and countercharges hurled by the opposing sides against one another immediately before the eruption of the war, whereas πρόφασις, which Thucydides defines as "less often advanced" or better: "less prominent than any other in what

---

[1] Thuc. I.23.6. Representative of most translations is that of C.F. Smith in the Loeb Classical Library (*Thucydides* I [London and Cambridge, MA, 1928]) 43: "The truest explanation, although it has been the least often advanced, I believe to have been the growth of the Athenians to greatness, which brought fear to the Lacedaemonians and forced them to war. But the reasons publicly alleged on either side which led them to break the truce and involved them in the war were as follows."

[2] There is no reason to rehearse in detail here what are by now familiar issues. For the most important contributions, see especially K. Deichgräber, "Πρόφασις. Eine terminologische Studie," *Festschrift Max Wellmann zum 70. Geburtstag* (= *Quellen und Studien zur Geschichte der Naturwissenschaften und der Medizin* 3) (Berlin, 1933) 209-25; L. Pearson, "*Prophasis* and *Aitia*," *TAPA* 83 (1952) 205-23; G.M. Kirkwood, "Thucydides' words for 'cause'," *AJP* 73 (1952) 37-61; S. Schuller, "About Thucydides' use of αἰτία and πρόφασις," *Revue Belge de Philologie* 34 (1956) 971-84; C. Schäublin, "Wieder einmal πρόφασις," *MH* 28 (1971) 133-44; H.R. Rawlings III, *A Semantic Study of Prophasis to 400 B.C.* (= *Hermes* Einzelschrift 33) (Wiesbaden, 1975).

was said" (ἀφανεστάτην δὲ λόγῳ), is "the truest," that is, the explanation which comes closer than any other to the historical reality Thucydides promises to present.

When it comes to identifying in concrete terms, however, what Thucydides meant by ἀληθεστάτη πρόφασις, there are serious disagreements among scholars. By far the most influential interpretation in our generation, which still dominates the thinking of 'modernists' and 'post-modernists' alike,[3] has been Mme de Romilly's view that the ἀληθεστάτη πρόφασις is unequivocally Athenian imperialism: the pursuit of imperial power on the part of Athens rather than the specific incidents that produced increasing friction between Athens and the Peloponnesian League caused, in the opinion she attributes to Thucydides, the conflict between the two superpowers of fifth-century Greece.[4] Mme de Romilly does not go so far as to take τοὺς Ἀθηναίους alone as the subject of ἀναγκάσαι, which would saddle the Athenians exclusively with the responsibility for the war. But she pays attention to only one of the two participles that modify τοὺς Ἀθηναίους, and that will not do. Imperialism can indeed be read into Thucydides' statement by taking μεγάλους γιγνομένους with τοὺς Ἀθηναίους. But one does not have to deny the unquestionable importance Thucydides sees in Athenian imperialism as contributing to the genesis of the Peloponnesian War to recognize that this interpretation gets at only half of what Thucydides asserts. In his eyes, the war was brought about not only by "the growth of the Athenians to greatness," but equally by the fear this growth instilled in the Lacedaemonians (καὶ φόβον παρέχοντας τοῖς Λακεδαιμονίοις).

Accordingly, other scholars have tried to redress the balance by giving due weight to Spartan fears in their interpretations of what Thucydides may have meant by ἀληθεστάτη πρόφασις.[5] Yet all these interpretations and most of the translations of the passage in question are flawed in one important respect.

---

[3] For a definition of these approaches, see W.R. Connor, "A post-modernist Thucydides?," *CJ* 72 (1977) 289-98; cf. also "Thucydides," in *Ancient Writers: Greece and Rome* I, ed. by T.J. Luce (New York, 1982) 267-89, esp. 282-86.

[4] J. de Romilly, *Thucydide et l'impérialisme athénien* (Paris,1947) 23 with n. 3 (= *Thucydides and Athenian Imperialism*, 2nd ed. tr. by P. Thody [Oxford, 1963] 18 with n. 3); cf. also A.G. Woodhead, *Thucydides on the Nature of Power* (Cambridge, MA, 1970).

[5] See, for example, G.E.M. de Ste. Croix, *The Origins of the Peloponnesian War* (London, 1972) 60-62, 290-92; C. Schneider, *Information und Absicht bei Thukydides* (= *Hypomnemata* 41) (Göttingen, 1974) 105-110; T.E. Wick, "A note on Thucydides 1.23.6 and ἡ ἀληθεστάτη πρόφασις," *AC* 44 (1975) 176-83; K.J. Dover in *HCT* 5 (1981) 415-23; M. Cogan, *The Human Thing: The Speeches and Principles of Thucydides' History* (Chicago, 1981) 8, 135, 192; P.J. Rhodes, "Thucydides on the causes of the Peloponnesian War," *Hermes* 115 (1987) 154-65 *passim*.

THE PROBLEM OF THUCYDIDES I.23.6

In speaking of Sparta's being 'forced' into the war and by translations such as "the truest explanation I believe to have been the growth of the Athenians to greatness, which brought fear to the Lacedaemonians and forced them to war,"[6] or "c'est à mon sens que les Athéniens, en s'accroissant, donnèrent de l'appréhension aux Lacédémoniens, les contraignant ainsi à la guerre,"[7] they ignore the fact that there is no word for 'them' or 'les' in Thucydides' text at I.23.6; i.e. they fail to note that ἀναγκάσαι lacks a direct object. This would of itself not be disturbing, since a direct object might be extrapolated from the preceding Λακεδαιμονίοις. This is the way chosen by Alfred Croiset in his edition of 1886: "Avec ἀναγκάσαι il faut suppléer αὐτούς, représentant les Lacédémoniens, et sous-entendu, suivant l'usage grec, avec le second verbe."[8] But this means not only to inject into the text something that is not there, but also to assume arbitrarily that the compulsion to go to war existed, in Thucydides' view, only for the Spartans. That this cannot be so is shown by a number of considerations. In the first place, Croiset's interpretation conveys the impression that Athenian intimidation provoked the Lacedaemonians into declaring war. If that had been Thucydides' meaning, we should have expected him to use the aorist participle γενομένους to describe Athenian growth as a *fait accompli* which intimidated the Spartans, and perhaps also an infinitive in place of the participle παρέχοντας. However, the fact that he uses two present participles and connects them with a καί shows that the process of Athenian growth had the development of Lacedaemonian fears as a concomitant, that, in other words, growing Athenian power gave *ipso facto* rise to Spartan apprehension. If an αὐτούς were to be supplied, it would, therefore, have to apply to both Athenians and Spartans; the fact that it is omitted makes the emphasis fall heavily on ἀναγκάσαι. Growth and fear combine to create the necessity of war.

This interpretation receives some support from the only two other Thucydidean passages in which an active form of the verb ἀναγκάζω lacks a direct object. At II.75.3, ἠνάγκαζον ἐς τὸ ἔργον states that Lacedaemonian ξεναγοί exerted pressure to complete the siege works against Plataea. The context here makes it clear that the pressure is exerted on the soldiers who participated in the siege of Plataea; but the absence of an αὐτούς to make this explicit shifts the emphasis onto the urgency to complete the siege works. Again, at V.31.3, ἐπηνάγκαζον tells merely of the pressure for payment of arrears which Elis applied on Lepreum. The fact that there is no αὐτούς to make its application to

---

[6] See n. 1 above.

[7] J. de Romilly (ed. & tr.), *Thucydide, La guerre du Péloponnèse* I (Paris, 1953) 16.

[8] A. Croiset (ed.), *Thucydide, Histoire de la guerre du Péloponnèse. Texte grec, Libres I-II* (Paris, 1886) 179.

Lepreum explicit places the emphasis on the pressure itself rather than on those to whom it is applied.

While these passages support, but do not constitute a decisive demonstration of our interpretation of I.23.6, Thucydides' statement on the ἐς τὸ φανερὸν λεγόμεναι αἰτίαι—"the reasons publicly alleged"—which follows his definition of the ἀληθεστάτη πρόφασις clearly indicates that both sides for their own reasons dissolved the Thirty-Years' Peace. This means that Thucydides did not regard the war as a preventive war, which the Lacedaemonians felt themselves compelled to undertake, but that he recognized that the Athenians, too, had reasons to renounce the peace treaty. Accordingly, the ἀληθεστάτη πρόφασις is neither the growth of Athens nor the fear engendered in Sparta in isolation one from the other, but the insight that the development of Athenian power and the fear this instilled in Sparta made the outbreak of war a necessity. This necessity is its focus, not the mere growth of Athenian power, nor the concomitant development of Sparta's fear, nor again the priority of the one over the other. Thucydides' point is that the progressive growth of Athenian power and the resulting fear among the Lacedaemonians created the ἀνάγκη to go to war, and it is this ἀνάγκη which is, in his view, the truest explanation of the war. He does not state at this point that either the growth or the fear was the result of necessity; his contention is that their existence created a situation of which war was the necessary consequence. It follows from this that Thucydides regarded it as his task as a historian not to confine himself to reporting the ἐς τὸ φανερὸν λεγόμεναι αἰτίαι—"the reasons publicly alleged"—but especially to bringing out into the open what had remained ἀφανεστάτη λόγῳ, namely that the sequence of events which led to the outbreak of hostilities followed a necessary course, which was in itself not self-evident. Two translations seem to me to capture the essential point. One is Lorenzo Valla's of 1452: "Nam verissimam quidem sed minime sermone celebratam arbitror extitisse causam Athenienses magnos effectos et Lacedaemoniis formidolosos necessitatem imposuisse bellandi";[9] the other is Richard Crawley's: "The real cause I consider to be the one which was formally most kept out of sight. The growth of the power of Athens, and the alarm which this inspired in Lacedaemon, made war inevitable."[10]

If, then, it is correct to interpret Thucydides as meaning at I.23.6 that the truest explanation of the war was that it emerged as an ἀνάγκη from the events preceding it, it is first imperative to ascertain the precise meaning(s) in Thucydides of the verb ἀναγκάζω and its various forms and compounds, of the

---

[9] Laurentius Valla (ed.), *Thucydides: De Bello Peloponnesiaco* (Venice, 1480?) Bodl. Lib. Oxf. Auct. K.3.23,

[10] *The Complete Writings of Thucydides: The Peloponnesian War*, ed. by J.H. Finley, Jr. (New York, 1951) 15.

noun ἀνάγκη and of the adjective ἀναγκαῖος. Once we have established the uses of the ἀναγκ- stem, we shall have to consider in which of the several senses Thucydides may have regarded the outbreak of the Peloponnesian War as a necessity, and trace the course by which he tries to argue the truth of his point. After that, we shall examine to what extent ἀνάγκη informs the rest of Thucydides' History. Next, we shall investigate what light ἀνάγκη throws on Thucydides' view of the problem of morality in human affairs, and finally make a few remarks on Thucydides' thoughts on the usefulness of historical study.

Ch. II. The Connotations of Ἀνάγκη in Thucydides

Since our aim is to find out as precisely as we can what Thucydides had in mind when he stated that the growth of Athenian power and the fear it instilled in Sparta ἀναγκάσαι ἐς τὸ πολεμεῖν, our first question is what he may have meant by ἀναγκάσαι. Because the question concerns Thucydides' usage alone, we can afford to ignore the use other authors made of ἀνάγκη words, except to the extent that their usage may illuminate problems that cannot easily be answered on the basis of Thucydides' text alone.[1] Moreover, to substitute 'necessity' or a cognate term for every occurrence of an ἀνάγκη word will not do, since we cannot assume that the range of the English term is coextensive with the Greek. English 'necessity', its lexical definitions apart,[2] has a number of different connotations. It may be something foreordained by a divinity or predetermined by some transcendental and inscrutable force which man is powerless to resist. It may be inherent in our human condition, such as the necessity to breathe, eat, sleep, and eventually die; it may be thought of as inhering in the laws of the physical universe, such as gravity or the motion of the earth and the celestial bodies. It is usually regarded as inescapable, but there are also instances in which it is—or can be—avoided. For example, the payment of taxes is almost universally necessary; but what if a person forgets to pay or pays less than his share? Nothing may happen if the neglect remains undiscovered; much may happen if one is found out.

---

[1] A fresh systematic treatment of ἀνάγκη remains a desideratum, especially since its most recent full discussion in H. Schreckenberg, *Ananke: Untersuchungen zur Geschichte des Wortgebrauchs* (= *Zetemata* 36) (Munich, 1964) is seriously flawed in that it selects the ancient evidence to fit into a preconceived pattern.

[2] *Webster's Third New International Dictionary* (1961) divides its principal meanings in three: (1) the quality or state or fact of being necessary; (2) the quality or state or fact of being in difficulties or in need; and (3) something that is necessary: requirement, requisite. Of these, (1) has four subsections: (a) a condition arising out of circumstances that compels a certain course of action; (b) inevitableness, unavoidability; (c) great or absolute need; indispensability; and (d) absence of physical or moral liberty: physical or moral compulsion; constraint or compulsion arising out of the natural constitution of things, impossibility of a contrary order or condition of things.

Which of these attributes and connotations does ἀνάγκη have in Thucydides? There has been, to the best of my knowledge, only one scholarly attempt so far to find an answer to this question by examining all 161 Thucydidean passages containing ἀνάγκη words, that of Christoph Schneider in his monograph *Information und Absicht bei Thukydides* (1974).[3] Its most important conclusion is unimpeachable: there is not a single instance in Thucydides of a mysterious or inscrutable ἀνάγκη. All ἀνάγκαι, whether expressed by verb, noun, or adjective, in speeches or in narrative, are intelligible and rationally explicable. None is predetermined either by a divinity or by some transcendental force. But his many astute and valid observations are so vitiated by selective interpretation to confirm preconceived ideas that it seems desirable and even necessary to look at the evidence once again to try to let it speak for itself,[4] tiresome though the process may be.

The least avoidable ἀνάγκαι are those imposed by external factors over which man has no control. But that does not mean that they are not intelligible and identifiable. For example, when we are told that the crammed quarters at Pylos—its στενοχωρία—compelled the Athenian troops under Demosthenes to take their meals at the extreme ends of Sphacteria (IV.30.2), the compulsion is caused by unalterable geographical factors, the consequences of which could, under the circumstances, only have been that the soldiers either should consume their food in discomfort or refrain from eating altogether. Obviously either alternative would have been unacceptable to them, especially since in their view a more comfortable place was available. In short, the geographical constraint, while avoidable in absolute terms but only under impossible conditions, was not avoidable in the view of those affected by it. Similar considerations apply to two passages in which climatic conditions constitute the ἀνάγκη in one, a storm compels Mindarus to make an unplanned landing at Icarus (VIII.99.1); in

---

[3] Schneider (above, Ch. I n. 5) 102-110. J. de Romilly, "La notion de nécessité dans l'histoire de Thucydide," in *Science et Conscience de la Société. Mélanges en l'honneur de Raymond Aron* I (Paris, 1971) 109-28, counts only 102 ἀνάγκη words in Thucydides (p. 118), but does not base her discussion on their usage. The conclusions of de Ste. Croix (above, Ch. I n. 5) 61 with n. 26, although based on a citation (but without discussion) of only 27 of these 161 passages, are uncritically accepted by Dover (above, Ch. I n. 5) 420 n. 1, and by W.R. Connor, *Thucydides* (Princeton, 1984) 32 n. 31.

[4] For example, Schneider's assertion that ἀνάγκη has an apologetic tendency in every speech in which it occurs (103) simply does not tally with the facts: in 16 out of the total of 30 uses of ἀνάγκη in speeches no trace of defensiveness can be detected; further, it is difficult to discover the basis for his assertion that ἀνάγκη "wird von Thukydides immer nur dann konstatiert, wenn es Handlungen und Ereignisse zu erklären gilt, die nach bestimmten Kriterien anders hätten verlaufen sollen" (107), especially since these criteria are nowhere defined. While these and similar inadequacies affect S.'s final definition of ἀνάγκη, they impair the total value of his work only in minor ways.

the second we are told that it is more usual for the Corcyraeans to receive foreign ships driven into their harbor by ἀνάγκη than to sail out to seek foreign contacts (I.37.3). Thucydides does not specify what might constitute an ἀνάγκη of this kind. But stormy weather must surely be included among the compelling factors, and other emergencies, such as lack of food and water or the need of repair, may also be reasons. Here, too, uncontrollable sources bring about the compulsion: the alternatives of shipwreck or death at sea are intolerable for those involved, but the point at which their situation becomes intolerable can only be determined by their judgment, which, however, becomes objectively valid since Thucydides implies that those whose help is sought accept it as reasonable. There are, further, two external ἀνάγκαι from whose objective validity the Spartans seem to be exempted: in connection with the surrender of the Spartan troops on Sphacteria, Thucydides remarks that his Greek contemporaries thought that no hunger or any other ἀνάγκη would ever have induced the Spartans to give up their arms (IV.40.1), and he attributes to the Melians the confidence that considerations of kinship would compel the Spartans to come to their aid (V.104). In neither case do the Spartans respond as expected: at Sphacteria they do surrender, and they leave the Melians in the lurch. Can we infer from these two passages that there are cases in which ἀνάγκη can be avoided? Such a conclusion would be erroneous. The context makes it clear that, while objectively speaking hunger and emergency situations are a sufficient compulsion for most people to surrender, the Spartans are hardier than most people; and that while objectively kinship is a compelling reason to come to the aid of a state in need, the Spartans are more callous or the Melians more naive than most people. In other words, these two passages only demonstrate that not all ἀνάγκαι need to be perceived as such by all people.

Thucydides treats historical events, too, as imposing external ἀνάγκαι. They account, for example, for the development of the Athenian as well as a Sicilian navy. In the case of Athens, the ἀνάγκη came from the Persian invasion (VII.21.3); in the case of Sicily, it developed as a result of the Athenian invasion (VIII.2.3). Reasonable responses to emergency situations, not any transcendent pressures, made the creation of both navies inevitable, since defeat would have been the only alternative. Finally, an externally imposed ἀνάγκη can be attributed to the principle, often encountered in Thucydides, that "actions speak louder than words."[5] At the Congress of Gela, Hermocrates says that the Athenian presence in Sicily will be a more cogent argument for Sicilian unity than his speech can be (IV.60.1), and Brasidas invites the trust of the Acanthians by telling them that the actions which follow Spartan professions create the necessary conviction that their interests lie exactly where they say

---

[5] The tragic aspect of the λόγος/ἔργον antithesis has its classic exponent in Adam Parry's Logos *and* Ergon *in Thucydides* (diss. Harvard, 1957) (Salem, NH, 1981), esp. 62-89.

their interests lie (IV.87.1). Although in both instances the deeds involved cannot yet be unavoidable since they lie in the future, what matters linguistically is that they are claimed by the speakers to be inescapable.

A second group of ἀνάγκαι consists of minimum requirements of one sort or another, in which the compulsions are dictated by the need to survive or to preserve something essential to those involved. Enough food for survival is the ἀνάγκη for the migratory gatherers of the earliest times in Greek history (I.2.2), for the besieged Potidaeans (II.70.1), and for Demosthenes' troops in Sicily (VII.82.2). Minimum military needs are at stake when Themistocles marks time as an ambassador in Sparta until notified that the wall has reached the minimal height for the defense of Athens (I.90.3); when Brasidas wants to hide from his Athenian opponents at Amphipolis the inadequate equipment and number of his troops (V.8.3); and when Athenagoras disparages the puny tents and inadequate equipment of the Athenian invaders of Sicily (VI.37.2). Minimal actions are described as ἀνάγκαι in Nicias' warning to his retreating troops to engage in fighting only when necessary (VII.81.3); in the Corinthian reproach to the Spartans that they lack the most basic military and political enterprise (I.70.2); and in the "basic and less than adequate" exhortation Nicias addresses to his troops before the battle in the Great Harbor (VII.69.3). From the standpoint of those affected, there is no viable alternative and no escape from these ἀνάγκαι.

On the face of it, the least unavoidable constraint is that which a speaker feels to respond to a point made by an earlier speaker or to make a point which, he believes, his situation requires. For example, in light of the points made by the Corcyraeans in their request for an alliance with Athens, the Corinthians feel compelled not only to express their opinion on the possible consequences of acceptance but also to defend themselves against the charge of having launched an unjustified attack on their colony (I.37.1). Obviously, by no objective standard would the world have come to an end if the Corinthians had failed to justify their actions, yet they could not have done so without seriously jeopardizing the desired effect of their speech; hence it was unavoidable for them to address this issue. The same is true of the constraint the Melians felt to adopt an argument from expedience in view of the groundrules laid down by the Athenians against arguments from morality (V.90); it is also true of the necessity felt by Alcibiades to respond to the aspersions cast by Nicias upon his competence to command (VI.16.1), and of Euphemus' feeling that he had to defend the legitimacy of the Athenian empire against Hermocrates' attack on it (VI.82.1).

The Athenian ambassadors addressing the First Lacedaemonian Congress regard it as necessary to rehearse once more those events of the Persian Wars which led to the acquisition of Athenian power, even though no previous speaker had referred to them and even though they, as well as their audience, would willingly dispense with this litany (I.73.2). Nevertheless, they believe that their situation demands that they address themselves to an issue whose omission would prove detrimental to their cause. Objectively more compelling is the constraint felt by Alcibiades in Sparta to begin his speech by dispelling the prejudice against him, since he could not hope otherwise to gain a favorable hearing (VI.89.1). Finally, there belongs in this group the pathetic peroration of the Plataeans before the Spartan judges, in which they deplore the necessity that their speech must come to an end, since with it the risk to their lives draws closer (III.59.3). The necessity to end a speech is absolute, as no one can go on speaking forever, but the underlying tone also intimates that the outcome, though still avoidable as lying in the future, will be a foregone conclusion in the mind of the speakers.

Since Thucydides' subject is a war, the presence of military ἀνάγκαι in greater number and variety than any other is not surprising. Conscripted citizen soldiers, we may presume, serve under the ἀνάγκη of social pressures, because the alternative would be disgrace or worse incurred through social disapprobation, but they can still be regarded as serving voluntarily when contrasted with mercenaries (VII.48.5), inasmuch as pay is not their motive in going to war. The only ἀνάγκη under which mercenaries labor is to be detailed to tasks for which they have no taste: ἀναγκαστός describes mercenaries pressed into naval service by Nicias, who abscond to their various cities at the earliest opportunity (VII.13.2); it also describes the registered hoplites made to serve as marines by Leon and Diomedon, a function normally assigned to the socially inferior thetes (VIII.24.2). A service regarded as unavoidable is also the ἀνάγκη in Thucydides' statement about the intent of Nicias' second speech before the Sicilian Expedition, namely that he "thought that, by dwelling on the magnitude of the enterprise, he would either dissuade the Athenians (from undertaking it), or, if compelled to join it, would do everything possible to ensure its safety" (VI.24.1).

In the field, the execution of a task assigned by a commanding officer becomes ἀνάγκη for those to whom it has been assigned: Spartan ξεναγοί press for the completion of the siege works against Plataea (II.75.3); Brasidas, in attempting to intercept Demosthenes' attack on Pylos, makes his helmsman run his ship ashore (IV.12.1); Hermocrates' proposal for military reform in Syracuse includes compulsory training for new troops (VI.72.4); during a lull in the fighting against Syracuse, Nicias makes his trierarchs refit their ships (VII.38.2); and in the last moment of despair, when the Syracusans have blocked the Great Harbor, the Athenians compel all men of military age to man their ships (VII.60.3). The same applies to non-military personnel drafted into service with the army: we hear of bakers (VI.22.1) and of one hundred boats (VI.44.1) requisitioned to join the Sicilian campaign, and of foodsellers compelled by the Syracusans to take their goods to the shore for sale, in order to enable the ships' crews to spend less time over their meals (VII.39.2). Disobedience, in all these cases the only alternative to the ἀνάγκη imposed, would have intolerable consequences for those involved, so that the constraint imposed by the order becomes inescapable for them.

Treaty obligations or threat of superior force constitute military ἀνάγκαι in relations between states. Especially informative in this respect is Book VII, chapter 57, where we get an impressive array of allies fighting under various kinds of constraint on the opposing sides in Sicily. The list shows, according to Thucydides, that advantage (τὸ ξυμφέρον) or ἀνάγκη were more potent factors for fighting on one side or the other than considerations of justice or kinship (VII.57.1): 'advantage' probably refers to mercenaries fighting for whatever side would pay the highest price or perhaps to states that regarded the expedition to be to their advantage. Ἀνάγκη, as we shall see, seems to apply to those whom treaty obligations of their home states constrained to serve. Contrasted with the Athenians and some Ionians who came of their own free will (VII.57. 2: ἑκόντες)—though in another context their service had been identified as δι' ἀνάγκης to contrast it with the mercenaries in the service of Syracuse (VII. 48.5)—other Ionians came along constrained not by ties of kinship but of treaty obligations and as subjects of Athens (VII.57.4); Aeolians from Methymna, Tenedos, and Aenia were constrained to fight against their Boeotian kinsmen, who were allied with Syracuse (VII.57.5); ἀνάγκη made Dorian states, such as Rhodes and Cythera, fight against the Spartans under Gylippus on the Syracusan side, and Rhodians and Argives against their colonists at Gela (VII.57.6). Of the Dorian Corcyraeans Thucydides says that they fought against the Syracusans and Corinthians, though kinsmen of the former and colonists of the latter, "alleging compulsion, but in fact no less from desire because of their hatred of the Corinthians" (VII.57.7). Internal ἀνάγκαι compelled the people of Thurii and Metapontum to fight alongside Athens (VII.57.11); in the case of the Sicyonians, the imposition by Sparta of an oligarchical regime at Sicyon (V. 81.2) constrained them to fight on the side of Syracuse(VII.58.3).

While the ἀνάγκαι under which allies of the two sides fought in Sicily are viewed from the perspective of those affected by them, another set of ἀνάγκαι is seen from the vantage point of those who impose or manipulate them for their own ends. In some cases, ἀνάγκη will have embodied force or the threat of force by a superior power over men for whom resistance would have spelled disaster or death. So, for example, the pressures the Athenians brought to bear upon their allies in the Delian League to pay tribute and supply ships and military service (I.99.1), or those through which Agis exacted hostages and money from Achaea Phthiotis and other Thessalian dependencies in 413 B.C. (VIII.3.1). We encounter them also in the belief of the Athenian troops on Samos that control of the navy gave them the means of exacting financial contributions from the allies (VIII.76.4), and in the resumption of payment of a talent owed to Zeus enforced by the people of Elis on Lepreum (V.31.3). Moreover, the compound προσαναγκάζω regularly appears to describe the coercing of others into joining military operations already in progress, for example, in the successful Athenian attempts to bring recalcitrant Sicels over to their side (VI.88.5), in Alcibiades' advice to the Spartans to have a Spartan organize an army of Sicilians in Sicily and to make those join who refuse to do so voluntarily (VI.91.4), and in the statement that the Spartans made the other Peloponnesians join them in sending reinforcements to Sicily (VII.18.4). Ἀνάγκαι of this sort can also result in subjugation: the fact that the friendly Acarnanians had already subjugated Oeniadae (IV.77.2) made it easy for Demosthenes to control it, and the Melians' refusal to submit to Athens resulted in military pressure and the ravaging of their land (V.84.2).

Closely related to these are ἀνάγκαι manipulated by skillful deployment of forces at one's disposal for military or diplomatic ends, which we may call 'strategems'. The verb ἀναγκάζω is used twice of the Corinthians coerced by Phormio's skill to fight a sea battle into which they did not want to be drawn (II.83.1 and 3); Brasidas bides his time before Amphipolis until circumstances compel Cleon to act as Brasidas had expected (V.7.1); at Epipolae, Nicias is compelled to reckon with the wall the Syracusans have erected (VII.6.1); and the Syracusans want to force the Athenians into an early sea battle in a position favorable to themselves to prevent the enemy's escape (VII.51.1). Examples of military ἀνάγκαι deployed for diplomatic ends are: the Spartans compel the Phocians to an agreement to give up a conquered town in Doris (I.107.2); the Athenians compel the people of Mylae to surrender and join them in an attack on Messina (III.90.3). This ἀνάγκη appears with a negative prefix in the speech of the Spartans who had come to Athens to negotiate the fate of the prisoners of Sphacteria and to offer peace: bitter enmities, they argue, are not securely settled by humiliating an opponent militarily and compelling him to swear to an unfair treaty, but by a fair treatment and less harsh terms than he had expected (IV.19.2). An opposite course of action is that proposed by Brasidas to the Acanthians: if, he asserts, they refuse to be compelled against their will to accept the freedom he offers, he will try to coerce them violently by ravaging their land (IV.87.2), and in one of his rare speculations on what might have been, Thucydides states that if the Spartans had followed up their victory off Euboea with greater daring, they would have compelled the Ionian fleet, though hostile to the oligarchy, to return home to defend Athens (VIII.96.4). In all these examples, predominantly military pressures are consciously applied by one party as sufficiently unavoidable ἀνάγκαι for the other to produce the desired effect.

Ἀνάγκαι appear as manipulated also in diplomatic or political situations, except that the way in which they are applied often remains obscure. This is well illustrated in Thucydides' account of Theseus' synoecism, described as ἠνάγκασε μιᾷ πόλει χρῆσθαι (II.15.2), in which the means of coercion remains unidentified and the question of the extent to which the cities of Attica could or could not have resisted the pressures he brought to bear on them unanswered. Only the lasting success of Theseus' achievement indicates that he accomplished the inevitable. Cleon regards as punishable only revolts initiated voluntarily by Athens' subject allies; those compelled by enemies of Athens are forgivable (III.39.2). Since we are not told what form such compulsion would have taken, the allies must have been unwilling to revolt but unable to resist the pressures brought to bear on them. The Plataeans, however, were able to resist Theban attempts to pressure them into joining the Boeotian League and went over to Athens instead (III.61.2). The use of the compound προσαναγκάζω shows that the ἀνάγκη here is viewed from the perspective of those who manipulated it, evidently in the mistaken belief that it would prove irresistible; but the imperfect indicates that its application remained no more than an attempt.[6] Similarly, the expected result of the treaty between Argos and Boeotia, promoted by Spartan ephors opposed to the Peace of Nicias, was to create a situation in which Boeotia would feel under little pressure to join the treaty with Athens (V.36.1). A diplomatic manoeuvre was employed here to prevent Boeotia from adopting an otherwise inevitable policy.

In internal politics, this kind of ἀνάγκη almost invariably appears in *stasis* situations and involves the use or threat of force: the Corcyraean oligarchs compelled ratification of their measures after having killed some sixty members of the Council (III.71.1); at Megara, the oligarchs staged a review of hoplites before compelling the people to cast an open ballot, so as to ensure the death penalty for collaboration with the Athenians (IV.74.3); oligarchy was forcibly imposed on Chios after its opponents had been executed on the charge of atticism (VIII.38.3); and the Athenian troops on Samos tried to pressure the oligarchical regime to return Athens to a democratic government and keep the πάτριοι νόμοι, while the oligarchs tried to make the troops accept an oligarchy (VIII.71.6). Here, too, ἀνάγκη is seen from the perspective of those imposing

---

[6] In all its eight occurrences in Thucydides the prepositional prefix in προσαναγκάζω assumes the existence of a policy or an institution which an agent tries to coerce someone into adopting. At IV.87.2-3, Brasidas promises the Acanthians that he will not compel anyone to come over to his side who does not want to; at V.42.2, we are told that any state that did not comply with the terms of the Peace of Nicias was to be coerced into conforming; at VI.72.4, Hermocrates proposes to enforce military training; at VI.88.5, the Athenians try to pressure the Sicels into joining them; at VI.91.4, Alcibiades suggests the formation of a Peloponnesian expeditionary force to be sent to Sicily, which any recalcitrants must be compelled to join; his proposal is implemented at VII.18.4; and at VIII.76.6, the Athenian forces on Samos try to coerce the oligarchs at home into obedience to the πάτριοι νόμοι. Cf. above, p. 13.

it and implies the belief that those manipulated will be constrained to act as desired.

Much more frequent, however, are those Thucydidean ἀνάγκαι not manipulated by human agents but arising from a given situation or a peculiar concatenation of circumstances. In military matters, a few examples will suffice. The initial success of the Corinthian navy against the Corcyraeans in the battle off the Sybota Islands prompts the Athenians to enter the action against the Corinthians (I.49.7). The siege of Potidaea and the arrival of Aristeus to help the besieged compel the Athenians to conclude an alliance with Perdiccas and to evacuate their troops from Macedonia (I.61.3). Phormio reminds his men before the battle of Naupactus of the advantage they enjoy over the enemy in their ability to choose the moment of battle and not to have a battle forced on them (II.89.6), and Nicias warns that the peace he negotiated is not secure, because the Spartans agreed to it from a position of weakness and circumstances compelled them (VI.10.2). Not surprisingly, however, by far the largest proportion of ἀνάγκαι arising from military situations are found in the account of the Sicilian campaign conveying the sense that the decision to undertake it created circumstances, especially for the Athenians, which they could no longer control. Only in one battle are the Syracusans affected, when, taken by surprise, they have to defend themselves in a hurry against an Athenian attack (VI.69.1). All other ἀνάγκαι weigh heavily upon the Athenians: they have to use all their ships for guard duty and can spare none for fighting (VII.13.1); they cannot replenish their crews and must replace their losses with their own men (VII.14.2); they are compelled to use Acarnanian and other mercenary archers and sharpshooters as crews for their ships (VII.60.4); the narrow space in the Great Harbor compels two or more ships to get entangled over one (VII.70.6) and in the *mêlée* the generals on either side give orders not to draw back unless absolutely necessary (VII.70.8). On their retreat, Nicias exhorts his troops that whenever they are compelled to fight for a piece of ground, they should fight for it as if it were their own fatherland (VII.77.5), and the tight order in which they are compelled to march causes them to fall and trample on each other when they reach the Assinarus River (VII.84.3). The inevitability of defeat conveyed by the accumulation of ἀνάγκη words must not blind us, however, to the fact that the situations which evoke them are invariably explicable in human and rational terms: there is nothing transcendent or mysterious about the necessities that bring about doom.

With our approach to diplomatic and political ἀνάγκαι arising from a concatenation of circumstances, we are also approaching a solution to the problem we set out to solve in Chapter I. The "Athenians growing great and presenting fear to the Lacedaemonians," which is given as the truest explanation of the "compelling into waging war" (ἀναγκάσαι ἐς τὸ πολεμεῖν) at I.23.6, refers, after all, not to a specific event but to a nexus of circumstances which, in

Thucydides' opinion, contained the seeds of war. We shall defer a discussion of those passages which he uses to prove his contention until the next chapter to concentrate here on a more general consideration of ἀνάγκαι created by a concatenation of circumstances. Some of these ἀνάγκαι beset individuals. For example, Themistocles, cornered in his flight from the Athenians, finds himself constrained to seek refuge with Admetus, King of the Molossians, with whom he was not on good terms (I.136.2). Surely, Themistocles' choice cannot have been dictated by an objective necessity, but since he himself seems to have been unable to envisage any other host more willing to receive him, we have to accept Thucydides' assertion that he had no viable alternative. Inherently more objective is Themistocles' explanation of his anti-Persian past in his letter to Artaxerxes as dictated by the ἀνάγκη to defend himself against the Persian attack on Greece (I.137.4). Thucydides describes Cleon as compelled by a situation in which, to advocate the blockade of Sphacteria, he would either have to agree with reports he had denounced, or be proved a liar (IV.27.4). No doubt, objectively speaking, other courses of action would have been open to him, but none would have been free from risks made inadvisable for him to take by his public position. So also the threat of the Spartan ambassadors who had come to Athens to negotiate the fate of the prisoners of Sphacteria: if the Athenians refused to consider their terms, personal enmity—no doubt engendered by the anticipated loss of their relatives—would necessarily develop in addition to public hostility. This is a diplomatic threat, which by its very nature cannot be objectively avoidable, but which the Spartans will nevertheless feel as inevitable for themselves (IV.20.1).

The ἀνάγκη that made it incumbent on Themistocles to seek refuge with Admetus has a public analogue in the statement of the Plataeans before their Spartan judges that they are taking a chance in making their speech, because "checkmated on all sides, we are constrained to take one course alone as safer than the rest, namely to say something" (III.53.3). The ἀνάγκη by which they feel constrained is explained in detail: none of their expectations in submitting themselves to Spartan judgment has been fulfilled; their judges are not impartial; no charges have been brought against them to answer; they have had to request permission to speak at all, and the one question they have been asked is designed to trap them. In other words, in the eyes of the reader their subjective feeling of entrapment appears as an objective and ineluctable reality. The factors inherent in ἀνάγκη are also enumerated in Thucydides' detailed narrative of the events which compelled the Mytilenaeans prematurely to revolt from Athens (III.2.1 and 4.2): their preparations for revolt, including negotiations for Boeotian and Spartan support, were reported to Athens by the people of Tenedos and Methymna as well as by Mytilenaeans friendly to Athens; subsequent Athenian protests were ignored and a fleet of forty ships was despatched against Mytilene; warned of their approach, the Mytilenaeans manned their half-finished walls and harbor installations, refused the demand to surrender, and were thus forced to fight a war (III.2.1-4.1). Every piece of information constitutes a step in an analysis of the objective circumstances which made a premature eruption of hostilities inevitable. Above all, we must not fail to notice the clarity (ἀκρίβεια) with which the constituent elements of each ἀνάγκη are laid bare. No obscurantist destiny blurs Thucydides' vision: at every stage the compulsion remains transparent and intelligible.

We must finally ask what factors in human experience cause ἀνάγκαι to develop. The answer to this question leads through an examination of a number of passages, mainly in speeches, which explicitly or by implication describe certain ἀνάγκαι as immanent in the human condition. The most general and perhaps most profound of these is put into the mouth of the Spartan king Archidamus: "It is wrong to believe that there is a great difference between one man and another, but it is right to believe that a superior person is he who is brought up to face the most essential constraints to which all men are subject" (I.84.4). My translation of this rather difficult passage is perhaps so free as to constitute an interpretation rather than a translation. But there can be no doubt that—presumably to counter the Corinthian contrast of Spartan and Athenian characteristics (I.70)—he denies any natural differences between one man and another, and affirms that an education aimed at recognizing basic ἀνάγκαι that apply to *all* men makes a person superior to others. Equally general in its thrust is Pericles' admonition during the Plague that Heaven-sent afflictions must be borne ἀναγκαίως, that is, in full awareness that they are unavoidable and that nothing can be done about them, but that afflictions due to enemy action must be faced with courage (II.64.2). Taken together these two statements may be used for our present purposes as affirming that the human condition as such is subject to ἀνάγκαι. More specific are Diodotus' assertion that "poverty gives men the courage of necessity" (as Crawley aptly translates) (III.45.4) and the Athenian argument (in answer to Boeotian complaints) that their disturbance of the sacred water at Apollo's temple at Delium was prompted by necessity and could therefore not be interpreted as a transgression (IV.58.5-6). Physical human needs constitute the ἀνάγκαι here, and they must also be thought of as underlying Nicias' exhortation to his troops that they have less reason to fear the enemy than their own straits and perplexity (VI.68.4). The psychological converse of this is his desperate admonition to his troops: there is no way out of their predicament but to be brave (VII.77.7).

War and subjugation are said to bring to the fore yet another set of human ἀνάγκαι. In connection with Thucydides' account of *stasis* on Corcyra we are told that it is part of the nature of men (φύσις ἀνθρώπων) to display better judgment in peace and prosperity, because they do not find themselves against their will confronted by the necessities war imposes on them (III.82.2); and elsewhere we learn that men would rather put up with violence, because it represents a constraint imposed by a superior power, than with injustice, which consists in being taken advantage of by an equal (I.77.4). Further, Pleistoanax's desire for peace is partly motivated by his belief that in wartime misfortunes are invariably attributed to the leaders (V.17.1).

We can sum up this part of our discussion as affirming that all men are subject to ἀνάγκαι; that constraints are imposed by poverty and physical wants; that the pressures of war bring out the worst in men through the deprivations to which they are required to resign themselves; that violence is more readily tolerated than injustice; and that leaders bear the brunt of failures. All these are characteristics of ἀνάγκαι affecting the individual. They are matched and extended by a set of public ἀνάγκαι. A shortage of food and lack of outside support compelled the Mytileneans to negotiate a surrender with Athens (III.27.1). The wartime situation compelled the Athenians to ignore religious sanctions and settle evacuees from the country in the Pelargikon (II.17. 1-2). In Pericles' view it is folly to go to war if there is a choice in the matter and if one is equally well off without it, but if a situation compels a choice between subjugation and survival, the person who does not opt for the latter invites censure (II.61.1). A parallel sentiment is attributed to the opposite side in the person of Hermocrates: no one is compelled to go to war in ignorance or is inhibited by fear from doing so (IV.59.2). But ἀνάγκαι are not always the same for all parties involved in a conflict. Pity, according to Cleon, must be shown only to equals, but not to those unequals who, because they cannot reciprocate it, are compelled by their situation to everlasting enmity (III.40.3); by arguing that in human reckoning (ἐν τῷ ἀνθρωπίνῳ λόγῳ) moral considerations are decisive only when the pressures that can be exerted by the two parties are equal, the Athenian ambassadors at Melos assume that different ἀνάγκαι apply to the strong than to the weak (V.89). The same distinction is implied in their statement that in human affairs it is a necessity imposed by nature invariably to rule whatever one controls (V.105.2), except that the ἀνάγκη that in the earlier statement applied only to the strong is now formulated in a way that eclipses and absorbs the ἀνάγκη weighing upon the weak. That Thucydides regarded this principle as universal is indicated by a statement given to Hermocrates on the opposing side: "it is just as much human nature invariably to rule those who submit, as it is to defend oneself against attack" (IV.61.5); there is no talk of ἀνάγκη here, but it is surely implied in πέφυκε, which echoes the φύσις ἀναγκαία of the Melian Dialogue. A final ἀνάγκη applicable to the strong rather than the weak appears in the Corinthian doctrine articulated at Sparta that in politics as in technology the most recent developments are of necessity superior, and in the conclusion drawn from it, namely that those states whose position compels them to be involved in many issues (which obviously means the stronger powers) need to put their efforts into innovation (I.71.3).

Much more could be said, but everything would corroborate two central points to be made about Thucydidean ἀνάγκαι. One is that all are intelligible and explicable in human terms and that there is nothing mysterious and obscurantist about them; the other that they exert compulsion only because those affected by them perceive no viable alternative course of action is open to them, because any alternatives theoretically or objectively available involve unacceptable consequences, such as death, defeat, surrender, or the like.[7] Applied to the ἀληθεστάτη πρόφασις passage (I.23.6), which was our point of departure, this means that the truest explanation of the outbreak of the Peloponnesian War was that the growth of Athenian power and the fear this evoked among the Lacedaemonians created a situation which left no viable alternative in human terms to either side but to go to war. To avoid war, the Athenians would have had to relinquish their imperial rule and the Spartans would have had to remain indifferent to Athenian expansion. Neither for Athens nor for Sparta would these alternatives have been acceptable or even possible: the war was inevitable, because both Athenians and Spartans realized that it was.

---

[7] Cf. the general discussion in K. von Fritz, *Die griechische Geschichtsschreibung* I (Berlin, 1967) 795-809, esp. 108: "Aber wenn Thukydides von ἀνάγκη spricht, meint er fast überall psychologischen Zwang."

Ch. III. Historical Method and the Necessity of the Outbreak of the Peloponnesian War

Two points follow from Thucydides' contention that the outbreak of the Peloponnesian War was an unavoidable necessity. The first is that he proposes at I.23.6 to deal with only those ἀνάγκαι which he saw inherent in the problems posed by growing Athenian power and Spartan fear, for obviously, these were the only ἀνάγκαι ascertainable to him. This is corroborated by the fact that his accounts of the past, the *archaeology* and the *pentekontaeteia*, contain no ἀνάγκη words in significant contexts.[1] This does not imply that Thucydides believed past history not to be governed by ἀνάγκαι; it implies only that past ἀνάγκαι cannot be reliably established. The past is all fact, and he lets the narrative itself establish what cogency the sequence of events may have had.

A second point follows from Thucydides' view of the ἀληθεστάτη πρόφασις. He saw the historian's task as consisting in constructing an account of the immediate antecedents of the Peloponnesian War without recourse to supernatural intervention or inscrutable transcendental forces. He knew that he had to demonstrate in intelligible human terms that human actions preceding the war contained a dynamic of their own, manifested in and generated by the concatenation of events, an ἀνάγκη—or better, a series of interdependent ἀνάγκαι—that explain these events and give them cohesion. He would not have been content to attribute, as Herodotus did, the fall of the Lydian empire to the expiation of a murder committed by a usurper five generations earlier,[2] or the accession of Darius to the neighing of a horse.[3]

To determine how Thucydides went about this task, some understanding of his general method is required. He gives his reader implicit or explicit informa-

---

[1] The single occurrence of ἀναγκαίου τροφῆς in the *archaeology* at I.2.2 refers to the minimum subsistence with which a gathering society was content. In the *pentekontaetaeia* ἀναγκαῖος occurs at I.90.3 to indicate the minimum height Themistocles wanted the walls to reach before proceeding with his negotiations at Sparta; at I.99.1, the Athenians are said to have applied ἀνάγκαι to recalcitrant allies; and at I.107.2 the Spartans coerce the Phocians in the First Peloponnesian War to come to an agreement to relinquish the towns they had captured in Doris.

[2] Hdt. I.8-86.1

[3] Id. III.85-86.

tion about some aspects of his procedure. On the collection of facts, the starting point of any historical inquiry, he is quite explicit: "As for the factual events of the war, I regarded it as my job to write them down not as I learned them from the first person who happened to come along, nor as they seemed to me, but both the events I experienced myself and those which I learned from others I thoroughly checked for accuracy in every detail to the extent that it was possible."[4]

But facts, however reliably established by an intelligent observer, rarely speak for themselves. In themselves they do not contain any ἀνάγκαι, that is, factors that cause further actions and events inevitably to develop. They need an interpreter to make them intelligible by deciding what is significant and what is not, which facts warrant inclusion and which do not. This interpreter can only be the historian. Thucydides is strangely silent on this aspect of his task, but there are unmistakable indications that he was aware of it. There is, for one thing, his emphasis on τεκμήρια and σημεῖα.[5] Though he speaks of them most prominently in connection with reconstructing the past in the *archaeology*, the principle of drawing inferences from the available evidence about what facts are important in reconstructing events or a sequence of events applies to the history as a whole. There is in addition his negative criticism of earlier historical accounts. For example, his censure: "so little pain do most people take over the search for truth, and they rather resort to what lies ready at hand,"[6] may be taken to indicate that his predecessors have not taken the same care he claims to have taken himself in ascertaining precisely what did happen and in sifting the relevant from the irrelevant. They were satisfied, he continues, with composing good stories for entertainment; they were not concerned to construct a cogent narrative acceptable to a rational audience desiring to learn from the past what sort of thing makes human beings act the way they do.[7] Although these words largely refer to Thucydides' procedure in reconstructing the past, it would be strange if he did not mean to apply them also to what was the present to him but would be the past to his readers.

The disclaimer, "nor as it seemed to me" (οὐδ' ὡς ἐμοὶ ἐδόκει, I.22.2), which Thucydides had used in his statement on the establishment of facts, is not applicable here, since judgments on significance or insignificance can only be

---

[4] Thuc. I.22.2: τὰ δ' ἔργα τῶν πραχθέντων ἐν τῷ πολέμῳ οὐκ ἐκ τοῦ παρατυχόντος πυνθανόμενος ἠξίωσα γράφειν, οὐδ' ὡς ἐμοὶ ἐδόκει, ἀλλ' οἷς τε αὐτὸς παρῆν καὶ παρὰ τῶν ἄλλων ὅσον δυνατὸν ἀκριβείᾳ περὶ ἑκάστου ἐπεξελθών. My interpretation is indebted to J.S. Rusten's forthcoming commentary on Thuc. II.

[5] See S. Hornblower, *Thucydides* (London, 1987) 100-107.

[6] Thuc. I.20.3: οὕτως ἀταλαίπωρος τοῖς πολλοῖς ἡ ζήτησις τῆς ἀληθείας, καὶ ἐπὶ τὰ ἑτοῖμα μᾶλλον τρέπονται.

[7] Ibid. 21 and 22.4.

the historian's own, whether he is aware of it or not. What were Thucydides' guidelines in selecting facts for their significance; what were his criteria? It is impossible to find a completely satisfactory answer to this question. In the first place, Thucydides is our only source for most of the facts recorded in his work: we have few facts from other sources, literary or epigraphical, against which to check or with which to supplement his. Second, Thucydides' account is too consistent, too much of a piece to be seriously disturbed by other evidence. Third, Thucydides' selection of facts is too deeply ingrained in his thinking habits, which pervade all his writing; since we find these habits pervading every part of his work, it is difficult to apprehend and define them.[8] The only help we get from him is the statement at I.23.6, which has served as our point of departure. If the ἀληθεστάτη πρόφασις of the outbreak of the Peloponnesian War is that, in view of the situation prevailing in the Greek world at the time, it was necessary for it to break out, we may assume that he selected his facts with a view to demonstrating this necessity. It is further reasonable to assume that the principle of selection applies not only to the events that precipitated the Peloponnesian War: it is to be expected that for his entire narrative of the war he selected those facts which seemed to him most essential to demonstrate a necessary concatenation in the sequence of all events which, after establishing them as such, he scrutinized for their significance.

Thucydides' account of the beginning of the Mytilenaean revolt, which we had occasion to discuss earlier,[9] gives us an insight into his general principles of selection. According to Thucydides, the Mytilenaeans were 'compelled' to revolt from Athens earlier than planned (III.2.1-4). Not only are the factors that explain the ἀνάγκη enumerated in considerable detail, but stylistically his narrative is framed by the use of ἀναγκασθέντες: at III.2.1 we read: ἀναγκασθέντες δὲ καὶ ταύτην τὴν ἀπόστασιν πρότερον ἢ διενοοῦντο ποιήσασθαι, and at III.4.2: ἀπαράσκευοι δὲ οἱ Μυτιληναῖοι καὶ ἐξαίφνης ἀναγκασθέντες πολεμεῖν. A different account is found in Aristotle's *Politics* (V.4, 1304a4-10). A wealthy Mytilenaean, Timophanes, had left two daughters as his heirs; when Dexandros, who was proxenos of Athens, failed to obtain these as wives for his sons, he fomented *stasis* and inveigled Athens to interfere. In itself this story is no less credible than the attribution of the English Reformation to the refusal of Pope Clement VII to annul Henry VIII's marriage to Catherine of Aragon. There is no reason to reject it out of hand as unhistorical,

---

[8] Although the battle between 'separatists' and 'unitarians' is largely quiescent at the present time (for a balanced survey, see K.J. Dover, "Strata of composition," in *HCT* 5 [1981] 384-444), I believe that even the separatists have not detected any profound change in Thucydides' thinking in the course of his work. For a full discussion, see O. Luschnat, "Thukydides der Historiker," *R.-E.* Suppl. 12 (1970) 1229-58. Cf. also J. Poullioux and F. Salviat, "Thucydide après l'exil et la composition de son Histoire," *Rev. Phil.* 59 (1985) 13-20.

[9] See pp. 16-17 above.

and it is not irreconcilable with Thucydides' account. Moreover, Thucydides may well have known this version; but if he did, he excluded it from his account on the grounds that not every fact is a significant fact. To mention, as one of several factors, that Mytilenaeans friendly to Athens informed the Athenians of what was going on in Mytilene makes his account more cogent and rationally acceptable than if he had given Dexandros' name and personal motives for calling in the Athenians. Meticulous about detail though he is, Thucydides concentrates on the essential and shuns the anecdotal.

A further point needs to be clarified. As we noted, one of the characteristics of ἀνάγκη in Thucydides is that it must be perceived as such by those it constrains. Consequently, in addition to establishing facts as facts and assessing their significance, Thucydides also had to show the view taken of them by contemporaries involved in the events, contemporaries who would make decisions arising from these events and at the same time shape the immediate future. The device he used was to include in his work speeches in which situations are viewed from the perspective of those implicated in them, in most cases antithetical speeches, to illuminate conflicting issues arising out of the same historical facts. It has always been universally recognized that speeches are a vital part of Thucydides' historiography. It has not been sufficiently emphasized, however, that they are a condition of his awareness of the role ἀνάγκη plays in human affairs. Since ἀνάγκαι depend for their existence on the perception of an agent, Thucydides must have the agents explain that, humanly speaking, no other acceptable course of action is open to them. Of the 161 ἀνάγκη words in Thucydides, 66, i.e., 41 percent, occur in speeches.

It is generally—and, I believe, correctly—taken for granted that the speeches are just as much Thucydides' own composition as is the narrative. It is equally true that he did not include—and could not have included—all the speeches which he knew were delivered in the period he covers. The principle of selectivity will have been in operation here at least as much as it was in winnowing out facts. Beyond the self-evident assumption that he included only what seemed significant to him, we can never know what criteria he employed for inclusion. To determine what Thucydides held to be significant, we get some help from his explicit statement about the speeches which he does include.[10]

---

[10] This is not the place to review the vast body of scholarly discussion of the speeches in Thucydides. A bibliography by W.C. West III up to 1973, included in P.A. Stadter (ed.), *The Speeches in Thucydides* (Chapel Hill, NC, 1973) 128-61, contains 351 items. The most important recent works to be added are: de Ste. Croix (above, Ch. I n. 5) 8-16; F. Egermann, "Thukydides über die Art seiner Reden und über Darstellung der Kriegsgeschehnisse," *Historia* 21 (1972) 575-602; Schneider (above, Ch. I n. 5) 143-54; Dover (above, n. 8) 393-99; D. Rokeah, "τὰ δέοντα περὶ τῶν αἰεὶ παρόντων. Speeches in Thucydides: factual reporting or creative writing?" *Athenaeum* 60 (1982) 386-401; J. Wilson, "What does Thucydides claim

After disclaiming any literal accuracy for them, both for himself and his informants,[11] he states that, contrary to the procedure followed in the establishment of facts, he exercised his own judgment in the composition of speeches by making the speakers say as precisely as possible what the factors objectively inherent in each situation demanded of each speaker.[12] This, it seems, is the sense of τὰ δέοντα, and the implication of this part of the statement is that Thucydides reserved for himself the judgment of what the issues really were. We can infer from this that the statement must *a fortiori* also apply to his decision about which speeches to include in his work: they would obviously only be speeches that addressed themselves to what he regarded to be the real issues in each given situation. If up to this point Thucydides conveys the impression that the speeches are free compositions to enable him to express his own views of what the true issues were—that, in other words, their content bears only a scanty resemblance to what a given speaker may actually have said on a given occasion—this impression is immediately eclipsed by the description of the checks Thucydides imposed on himself, which is contained in the rest of the sentence. He states that he adhered as closely as possible to the general thrust of the content of the speeches actually delivered.[13]

How does all this fit into our interpretation of Thucydides' view of the ἀληθεστάτη πρόφασις? If his aim was to give the truest explanation of the outbreak of the Peloponnesian War as the inevitable outcome of Athenian growth and Spartan fears, speeches of the kind he envisaged would be an indispensable tool in demonstrating his point. They would not only give him the opportunity to supplement his narrative by presenting the views of the foremost agents; they would also enable him to focus on what each speaker regarded as the real issues in a given situation (τὰ δέοντα) and to formulate the issues in his own way so as to bring out what ἀνάγκαι arising from them prompted the speaker to advocate the policy he did. It would also enable him to demonstrate the necessity, as he saw it, for the outbreak of the Peloponnesian War.

It remains to follow this last demonstration in detail to show how Thucydides saw the growing power of Athens and the fear it instilled in the Lacedaemonians combine in creating this necessity. Our text will be Book I, which poses and answers this question as the backdrop against which the events of the

---

for his speeches?" *Phoenix* 36 (1982) 95-103; and Hornblower (above, n. 5) 45-72.

[11] Thuc. I.22.1: χαλεπὸν τὴν ἀκρίβειαν αὐτὴν τῶν λεχθέντων διαμνημονεῦσαι ἦν ἐμοί τε ὧν αὐτὸς ἤκουσα καὶ τοῖς ἄλλοθέν ποθεν ἐμοὶ ἀπαγγέλλουσιν.

[12] Ibid.: ὡς δ' ἂν ἐδόκουν ἐμοὶ ἕκαστοι περὶ τῶν αἰεὶ παρόντων τὰ δέοντα μάλιστ' εἰπεῖν.

[13] Ibid.: ἐχομένῳ ὅτι ἐγγύτατα τῆς ξυμπάσης γνώμης τῶν ἀληθῶς λεχθέντων.

war itself must be seen. Thucydides' first step is to show in his account of the αἰτίαι the ἀνάγκαι inherent in the stages immediately preceding the war.

Four passages demonstrate how problems arising between Corcyra and Epidamnus resulted in open hostilities between Athens and Corinth. In the first of these, Thucydides reports in indirect speech that Corcyraean ambassadors warned the Corinthians that their continued support of Epidamnus would compel Corcyra to look for friends in quarters where they did not want to seek them.[14] Since this is a diplomatic threat of future retaliation for present provocation, we cannot regard the ἀνάγκαι as objectively unavoidable: other courses of action are still open to the Corcyraeans. However, their explicit disinclination to go to war with Corinth and their implicit refusal to countenance the present support Corinth is giving to Epidamnus leave them, they assert, no alternative but to prepare for the eventuality of armed confrontation by seeking allies wherever they can find them.

The second passage presents us with the second step in the concatenation of circumstances: Corcyraean ambassadors come to Athens and detail the situation, which they see as imposing an ἀνάγκη on them: "Since (after their earlier defeat) the Corinthians have embarked against us with a still larger force from the Peloponnese and the rest of Greece, and since we realize that we lack the power to survive with our strength alone, and further that we shall be in serious danger if subjugated by them, it is necessary to request help from you and everyone else."[15] In the view of the Corcyraeans, the size of the enemy fleet, their own isolation and weakness, and the danger of subjugation to Corinth combine to constitute a situation in which they cannot but turn for help to wherever they can hope to obtain it. Since they see no alternative open to them, the ἀνάγκη to request an alliance is unavoidable for them.

A third passage complements the other two in a most striking way in that it shows that ἀνάγκη constrains also the other side. The Corinthians who had come to Athens to oppose Corcyra's request for an alliance warn the Athenians that, if they should go along with Corcyra, the Corinthians would be compelled

---

[14] Ibid. 28.3: πόλεμον δὲ οὐκ εἴων ποιεῖν· εἰ δὲ μή, καὶ αὐτοὶ ἀναγκασθήσεσθαι ἔφασαν, ἐκείνων βιαζομένων, φίλους ποιεῖσθαι οὓς οὐ βούλονται ἑτέρους τῶν νῦν ὄντων μᾶλλον ὠφελίας ἕνεκα. The necessity to look for friends in undesirable quarters is echoed by Hermocrates at the Congress of Gela, IV.63.2: φίλοι μὲν ἂν τοῖς ἐχθίστοις, διάφοροι δὲ οἷς οὐ χρὴ κατ' ἀνάγκην γιγνοίμεθα.

[15] Id. I.32.5: ἐπειδὴ δὲ μείζονι παρασκευῇ ἀπὸ Πελοποννήσου καὶ τῆς ἄλλης Ἑλλάδος ἐφ' ἡμᾶς ὥρμηνται καὶ ἡμεῖς ἀδύνατοι ὁρῶμεν ὄντες τῇ οἰκείᾳ μόνον δυνάμει περιγενέσθαι, καὶ ἅμα μέγας ὁ κίνδυνος εἰ ἐσόμεθα ὑπ' αὐτοῖς, ἀνάγκη καὶ ὑμῶν καὶ ἄλλου παντὸς ἐπικουρίας δεῖσθαι.

to defend themselves against them as well as against the Corcyraeans.[16] As in the case of the earlier Corcyraean warning to Corinth, the necessity lacks absolute objective value, because it is a diplomatic threat of future action. The Corinthians could conceivably be so intimidated by the prospect of having to face the Athenian navy and the possibility that a confrontation would spell the end of the Thirty-Years' Peace that they might come to terms with Corcyra on the Epidamnus issue. But as a major naval power, Corinth cannot afford to let itself be intimidated: from her point of view there is no alternative but to fight Athens, if the Corcyraean alliance be accepted. In short, although in each case the necessity to act in a certain way is inevitable only for the party involved, the fact that both of the opposing parties feel the pressure to act as they propose excludes all alternative courses of action, and makes the resulting clash assume an aura of objective inescapability.

A fourth passage, not in a speech but part of Thucydides' narrative, shows how the ἀνάγκη, which had so far been only fears of future contingencies, became actualized in open hostilities. Although the Athenians had heeded the Corinthian warning to the extent of concluding only a defensive alliance with Corcyra (I.44.1: ἐπιμαχία), uncontrollable circumstances forced hostile action in the battle off the Sybota Islands. When the Corinthians routed the Corcyraean fleet and pursued it, "everyone got involved in the action and fine distinctions were no longer made: the situation came to the point that Corinthians and Athenians of necessity became embroiled with one another."[17]

'Ανάγκη words do not figure prominently in the narrative of the revolt of Potidaea, which followed hard upon the heels of the Corcyra affair and brought relations between Athens and Corinth to the breaking point.[18] Thucydides lets his detailed account of this most intricate situation explain its own dynamics, perhaps, we may surmise, because Potidaea was only the straw that broke the camel's back and added no essentially new factor to the explanation of growing hostilities between Athens and Corinth.

The next step is to explain how ἀνάγκαι, which had so far only developed into hostilities between Athens and a Peloponnesian power, came to involve the

---

[16] Ibid. 40.3: οὐ γὰρ τοῖσδε μόνον ἐπίκουροι ἂν γένοισθε, ἀλλὰ καὶ ἡμῖν ἀντὶ ἐνσπόνδων πολέμιοι· ἀνάγκη γάρ, εἰ ἴτε μετ' αὐτῶν, καὶ ἀμύνεσθαι μὴ ἄνευ ὑμῶν τούτους.

[17] Ibid. 49.7: ... τότε δὴ ἔργου πᾶς εἴχετο ἤδη καὶ διεκέκριτο οὐδὲν ἔτι, ἀλλὰ ξυνέπεσεν ἐς τοῦτο ἀνάγκης ὥστε ἐπιχειρῆσαι ἀλλήλοις Κορινθίους καὶ Ἀθηναίους.

[18] The adjective ἀναγκαίαν appears once in the eleven chapters that comprise this account (I.61.3) to describe a temporary ξυμμαχία concluded with Perdiccas to give the Athenians a free hand to cope with Potidaea and the Corinthians under Aristeus, who were coming to support her revolt.

Lacedaemonians. The scene is a congress of the Peloponnesian League convoked at Sparta on the Corinthians' initiative, because they believed that what they considered a breach of the Thirty-Years' Peace affected the entire Peloponnese (I.67.1). The speech of the Corinthian representatives aims at convincing the Spartans of the necessity to act that has been created by the present situation. To this end, they make three points: first, they accuse the Spartans of being content to keep what they have, of having no new ideas, and of never going as far as is necessary to go when it comes to action (καὶ ἔργῳ οὐδὲ τἀναγκαῖα ἐξικέσθαι, I.70.2); second, they assert that in politics as in technology the most recent developments are of necessity (ἀνάγκη) superior; and third, they draw from this the conclusion that states whose position compels them (ἀναγκαζομένους) to be involved in many issues need to put their efforts into innovation.[19] In short, they try to invite Spartan involvement in their relations with Athens by first censuring the Spartans for complacency in not seeing anything through to the conclusion demanded by the situation, by then pointing to the need for innovative policies, and by finally reminding them that the inevitable involvement of a major power in many issues requires new approaches. Concretely, the Corinthians go no further than to recommend a Spartan invasion of Attica to relieve Athenian pressure on Potidaea (I.71.4); the main thrust of what Thucydides makes them say is to arouse the Spartans to awareness of the same ἀνάγκαι which they—the Corinthians—see inherent in their own relations with Athens.

If the Corinthians present the Peloponnesian view of ἀνάγκη at this point, its counterpart is the speech of the Athenian ambassadors, who happened to be present on some other business at Sparta.[20] Thucydides has not prepared us for their presence, attributing it to mere chance. There is no reason to criticize him for this or to expect him to explain the necessity of their presence: the ἀνάγκη in which he is interested concerns the outbreak of the Peloponnesian War and the business necessitating the embassy had apparently nothing to do with that. But he uses the ambassadors' presence to give us the Athenian perspective on the ἀνάγκη which created that Athenian growth which, by inspiring fear in the Spartans, will have generated in its turn the conditions necessary for the outbreak of war.

Thucydides deliberately and explicitly joins the Athenian speech to the Corinthian in that he has the Athenians begin by stating that they regard it nec-

---

[19] Thuc. I.71.3: ἀνάγκη δὲ ὥσπερ τέχνης αἰεὶ τὰ ἐπιγιγνόμενα κρατεῖν· καὶ ἡσυχαζούσῃ μὲν πόλει τὰ ἀκίνητα νόμιμα ἄριστα, πρὸς πολλὰ δὲ ἀναγκαζομένοις ἰέναι πολλῆς καὶ τῆς ἐπιτεχνήσεως δεῖ. For the sentiment, cf. Euphemus at VI.87.2: πολλὰ δ' ἀναγκάζεσθαι πράσσειν, διότι καὶ πολλὰ φυλασσόμεθα.

[20] Id. I.72.1: τῶν δὲ Ἀθηναίων ἔτυχε γὰρ πρεσβεία πρότερον ἐν τῇ Λακεδαίμονι περὶ ἄλλων παροῦσα...

essary (ἀνάγκη) to state once more the steps by which Athens has acquired her present power (I.73.2). The necessity here cannot be objective in that no element in the situation constrained the Athenians even to participate in the deliberations of the Peloponnesian League. Nevertheless, because they believed, having listened to what the Corinthians had to say, that the situation required a justification of Athenian power, it was indeed necessary for them to speak up. They attribute the origin of their empire to the same Spartan indolence which the Corinthians had just blamed for a do-nothing policy *vis-à-vis* Athens: because the Spartans were disinclined to pursue the war against Persia to the bitter end, the Athenians accepted the leadership which the allies, at their own initiative, requested them to assume. From these foundations, the Athenians claim, fear, prestige, and self-interest compelled them (κατηναγκάσθημεν) to take the first steps toward developing their empire to its present strength.[21] It has long been recognized that we have here an explicit statement of some essential features of the dynamic which Thucydides himself saw inherent in the historical process,[22] especially in view of the role this unholy trinity plays throughout his work, in speeches as well as in his narrative. This is also shown in the claim he lets the Athenians make in the sequel about these three motivating forces. Appealing to the fact that the Spartans, too, base their leadership of the Peloponnese upon their own self-interest, the Athenians assert that, had they been in the place of Athens, the Spartans would have been compelled (ἀναγκασθέντες) to adopt the same imperious attitude toward the allies or else risk their survival.[23] The reason, they explain, is that to accept dominion when it is offered and not to relinquish it under the impact of prestige, fear, and self-interest is neither admirable nor alien to the way humans are.[24] The initial acquisition of dominion over others is, according to this thesis, not subject to the rules of necessity; once acquired, universal human motives, not confined to Athenians or Spartans, and consisting in fear, prestige, and self-interest, dictate its growth and its persistence. The growth of the Athenian empire which, in his statement of the ἀληθεστάτη πρόφασις, Thucydides had declared

---

[21] Ibid. 75.3: ἐξ αὐτοῦ δὲ τοῦ ἔργου κατηναγκάσθημεν τὸ πρῶτον προαγαγεῖν αὐτὴν ἐς τόδε, μάλιστα μὲν ὑπὸ δέους, ἔπειτα καὶ τιμῆς, ὕστερον καὶ ὠφελίας.

[22] See, most recently, A. Rengakos, *Form und Wandel des Machtdenkens der Athener bei Thukydides* (= *Hermes* Einzelschrift 48) (Stuttgart, 1984) 29-30; for prestige, see J. de Romilly, "Le thème du prestige dans l'œuvre de Thucydide," *Ancient Society* 4 (1973) 39-58.

[23] Thuc. I.76.1: καὶ εἰ τότε ὑπομείναντες διὰ παντὸς ἀπήχθησθε ἐν τῇ ἡγεμονίᾳ, ὥσπερ ἡμεῖς, εὖ ἴσμεν μὴ ἂν ἧσσον ὑμᾶς λυπηροὺς γενομένους τοῖς ξυμμάχοις καὶ ἀναγκασθέντας ἂν ἢ ἄρχειν ἐγκρατῶς ἢ αὐτοὺς κινδυνεύειν.

[24] Ibid. 76.2: οὕτως οὐδ' ἡμεῖς θαυμαστὸν οὐδὲν πεποιήκαμεν οὐδ' ἀπὸ τοῦ ἀνθρωπείου τρόπου, εἰ ἀρχήν τε διδομένην ἐδεξάμεθα καὶ ταύτην μὴ ἀνεῖμεν ὑπὸ τῶν μεγίστων νικηθέντων, τιμῆς καὶ δέους καὶ ὠφελίας. I see no need for Herwerden's insertion of τριῶν between ὑπὸ and τῶν.

to have created the conditions that made the war necessary, is now shown to have itself been the result of a necessity embedded in motivations common to all men. Thucydides shows later in his work how the operation of the same factors in Athenian imperialism, especially fear, was manifest in the Melian Dialogue, in Alcibiades' speech before the Sicilian expedition, and in Euphemus' defence of empire at Camarina.[25]

Thucydides attributes to Archidamus, introduced as ἀνὴρ καὶ ξυνετὸς δοκῶν εἶναι καὶ σώφρων ("a man reputed to be intelligent as well as level-headed"), the best in Spartan thinking on the issues raised by Corinth and Athens. While he agrees with the Corinthians that action needs to be taken, he also heeds the Athenian warning (I.78) that war must not be undertaken lightly. But most important for our present purposes is a contribution Thucydides has him make to the function of ἀνάγκη in human affairs: "It is wrong to believe that there is a great difference between one man and another, but it is right to believe that he is a superior person who is brought up to face the most essential constraints to which men are subject."[26] Archidamus refuses to accept the Corinthian contrast of Spartan and Athenian characteristics and adopts the Athenians' belief in the existence of universal human motivating forces. At the same time, however, he also believes that schooling is required to enable a person to recognize to which ἀνάγκαι he is to assign the highest priority. Archidamus' caution is overridden by Spartan impatience with Athenian conduct: fired by Sthenelaidas' appeal, the Spartans voted that the Thirty-Years' Peace had been violated and that war ought to be declared. The declaration of war itself, however, was postponed until a further meeting of the Peloponnesian League. In attributing this decision to fear of additional Athenian growth rather than to persuasion by Sparta's allies, Thucydides does not seem to intimate that the Corinthians' arguments lacked cogency, but that the Spartans gave greater weight to their own self-interest in reaching their decision. In identifying fear of further Athenian growth as their motive, Thucydides gives us the second element in the conditions underlying the ἀληθεστάτη πρόφασις, the necessity of war breaking out.[27]

The accounts of the First and Second Lacedaemonian Congress are interrupted by the *pentekontaeteia*, which provides the factual basis for the growth of Athenian power and Spartan fear between the end of the Persian and the outbreak

---

[25] See id. V.99; VI.18.3; 85.3; and 87.2.

[26] Id. I.84.4: πολύ τε διαφέρειν οὐ δεῖ νομίζειν ἄνθρωπον ἀνθρώπου, κράτιστον δὲ εἶναι ὅστις ἐν τοῖς ἀναγκαιοτάτοις παιδεύεται.

[27] Ibid. 88: ἐψηφίσαντο δὲ οἱ Λακεδαιμόνιοι τὰς σπονδὰς λελύσθαι καὶ πολεμητέα εἶναι οὐ τοσοῦτον τῶν ξυμμάχων πεισθέντες τοῖς λόγοις ὅσον φοβούμενοι τοὺς Ἀθηναίους μὴ ἐπὶ μεῖζον δυνηθῶσιν, ὁρῶντες αὐτοῖς τὰ πολλὰ τῆς Ἑλλάδος ὑποχείρια ἤδη ὄντα.

of the Peloponnesian War,[28] and thus supplies the underpinning for what had been only a general statement at I.23.6. Once this is recognized, the shortcomings for which this part of the work has so often been criticized become less glaring, though it would be claiming too much to say that they vanish altogether. We have already remarked that, though the *pentekontaeteia* expounds the conditions that created the ἀνάγκη for the outbreak of the Peloponnesian War, it contains no significant ἀνάγκη words because it deals with events antecedent to the κίνησις μεγίστη, which is Thucydides' theme.[29]

As soon as the narrative is over, however, its summary resumes the ἀνάγκη theme by stating the effect of the Athenian growth on the Spartans: "In the course of these fifty years, the Athenians consolidated their empire and greatly enhanced their own power. The Lacedaemonians, though aware of it, made only limited attempts to check them, and remained inactive for most of the time, as even before this they had never been quick to go to war, unless compelled (ἢν μὴ ἀναγκάζωνται), and partly because they were hampered by domestic wars, until Athenian power had clearly reached a height at which it began to encroach upon their league. At that point they regarded it as intolerable and decided to exert every effort to come to grips with it and to break its thrust, if they could, by embarking on this war."[30] The word 'fear' is not used, but it is clearly described as the motive that finally compelled Sparta to take the decisive step. The Second Lacedaemonian Congress, an account of which follows, has the Corinthians appeal to their fellow members of the Peloponnesian League that the point has been reached at which a vote for war is a necessity (ἐς ἀνάγκην ἀφῖχθαι, I.124.2). With the vote to go to war on this basis, Thucydides' own statement of the ἀληθεστάτη πρόφασις has been endorsed by one of the contending parties.

The endorsement by the other party follows an account of diplomatic bickering between Athens and Sparta that forms part of the αἰτίαι and διαφο-

---

[28] That this is the primary purpose of the *pentekontaeteia* is well brought out by P.K. Walker, "The purpose and method of 'the pentekontaetia' in Thucydides, Book I," *CQ* 51 (n.s. 7) (1957) 27-38. Less satisfactory is the treatment by R.A. McNeal, "Historical methods and Thucydides 1.103.1," *Historia* 19 (1970) 306-25, esp. 312-18.

[29] See n. 1 above.

[30] Thuc. I.118.2: ἐν οἷς οἱ Ἀθηναῖοι τήν τε ἀρχὴν ἐγκρατεστέραν κατεστήσαντο καὶ αὐτοὶ ἐπὶ μέγα ἐχώρησαν δυνάμεως, οἱ δὲ Λακεδαιμόνιοι αἰσθόμενοι οὔτε ἐκώλυον εἰ μὴ ἐπὶ βραχύ, ἡσύχαζόν τε τὸ πλέον τοῦ χρόνου, ὄντες μὲν καὶ πρὸ τοῦ μὴ ταχεῖς ἰέναι ἐς τοὺς πολέμους, ἢν μὴ ἀναγκάζωνται, τὸ δέ τι καὶ πολέμοις οἰκείοις ἐξειργόμενοι, πρὶν δὴ ἡ δύναμις τῶν Ἀθηναίων σαφῶς ᾔρετο καὶ τῆς ξυμμαχίας αὐτῶν ἥπτοντο. τότε δὲ οὐκέτι ἀνασχετὸν ἐποιοῦντο, ἀλλ' ἐπιχειρητέα ἐδόκει εἶναι πάσῃ προθυμίᾳ καὶ καθαιρετέα ἡ ἰσχύς, ἢν δύνωνται, ἀραμένοις τόνδε τὸν πόλεμον.

ραί (charges and disputes) and contains no significant ἀνάγκη words.[31] According to Thucydides, Pericles son of Xanthippus, "a man at that time the first of the Athenians and most influential in speech and in action," dispels any illusion that war can be averted. To the Lacedaemonian charges and demands he proposes equally unreasonable countercharges and counterdemands; on the basis of a realistic appraisal of the resources available to each side, he states: "we shall not start a war, but we shall defend ourselves against those who do: this is the right and dignified answer for our city to give. But we must be conscious of the fact that going to war is a necessity (εἰδέναι δὲ χρὴ ὅτι ἀνάγκη πολεμεῖν), and the more willing we are to accept it, the less harshly shall we feel the pressure of our adversaries; and that for both a city and an individual the greatest risks are the source of the highest prestige."[32] Here, toward the end of Book I, the circle opened near its beginning with Thucydides' statement of the ἀληθεστάτη πρόφασις has been closed. In showing through the mouth of the Corinthians that the necessity for war was perceived by the Peloponnesians, and through Pericles' mouth that the same necessity was recognized by the Athenians, Thucydides has given his own view the aura of objective truth. Moreover, through his detailed list of charges, countercharges, demands, and counterdemands he has shown that the necessity was avoidable, but only at a price neither side could accept. In their speech before the First Lacedaemonian Congress, the Athenians attributed the growth of their empire to the universally human motivations of fear, prestige, and self-interest. In the situation immediately preceding the outbreak of hostilities, neither side could have emphasized its own self-interest, but it is significant that the Corinthians predicate the ἀνάγκη for war on fear and Pericles on prestige. Ultimately, in Thucydides' eyes, it is the way the human animal is constituted that made the outbreak of the Peloponnesian War an inevitable necessity.

---

[31] For the ἀνάγκαι encompassing Themistocles in this passage (I.136.2 and 137.4) see above, p. 16.

[32] Thuc. I.144.2-3: ...πολέμου δὲ οὐκ ἄρξομεν, ἀρχομένους δὲ ἀμυνούμεθα.... εἰδέναι δὲ χρὴ ὅτι ἀνάγκη πολεμεῖν, ἢν δὲ ἑκούσιοι μᾶλλον δεχώμεθα, ἧσσον ἐγκεισομένους τοὺς ἐναντίους ἕξομεν, ἔκ τε τῶν μεγίστων κινδύνων ὅτι καὶ πόλει καὶ ἰδιώτῃ μέγισται τιμαὶ περιγίγνονται.

Ch. IV. Ἀνάγκη and the History of the Peloponnesian War

We can now approach the problem that is in some ways central to our inquiry as a whole: was Thucydides a determinist? Did he believe that the course of history is shaped by a concatenation of events over which man has no control or only such limited control that, however much he may plan and try to implement his plans, forces greater than he vitiate his intent and make him their victim? This problem has recently received a large share of scholarly attention by the so-called 'post-modernists',[1] and we shall try to see in this chapter and the next what contribution a study of ἀνάγκη can make toward providing an answer.

Our study of the ἀνάγκη that constitutes the ἀληθεστάτη πρόφασις for the outbreak of the Peloponnesian War enables us to make some preliminary observations. The fact that all ἀνάγκαι are transparent and capable of rational explanation shows that however much the outbreak of a war may have been determined, it was not determined by inscrutable transcendental forces. If we can isolate any factors in which ἀνάγκαι are anchored, we would have to identify them as the fear, prestige, and self-interest with which the Athenians explain the genesis of their empire and which they generalize into a universal principle (I.75-76). Does this justify our speaking of psychological determinism in Thucydides? Our observation that ἀνάγκαι can only operate if they are perceived as compelling by the agents involved in a particular situation, when combined with the fact that Thucydides' contention that the outbreak of the war was necessary is largely supported through his speeches, would indeed suggest

---

[1] The term 'post-modernist' was coined by Connor (above, Ch. I n. 3). It is based on a revival of interest in the views of F.M. Cornford, *Thucydides Mythistoricus* (London, 1907) under the influence of H.-P. Stahl's seminal *Thukydides: Die Stellung des Menschen im geschichtlichen Prozess* (= *Zetemata* 40) (Munich, 1966). Other important contributions are: A. Parry (above, Ch. II n. 4) and "Thucydides' historical perspective," *YCS* 22 (1972) 47-61; V.J. Hunter, *Thucydides the Artful Reporter* (Toronto, 1973); J.A. Grant, "Toward knowing Thucydides," *Phoenix* 78 (1974) 81-94; C. Schneider (above, Ch. I n. 5); L. Edmunds, *Chance and Intelligence in Thucydides* (Cambridge, MA, 1975); M. Cogan (above, Ch. I n. 5); H.R. Rawlings III, *The Structure of Thucydides' History* (Princeton, 1981); W.R. Connor, *Thucydides* (Princeton, 1984).

CHAPTER IV

that this is the case. However, this does not completely answer the question of determination, since we have also noted that ἀνάγκη words are almost entirely absent from such narrative portions as the *archaeology*, the *pentekontaeteia*,[2] the accounts of the Epidamnus affair[3] and of Potidaea,[4] and the three excursuses on the Cylonian revolt (I.126.2-127), on the end of Pausanias (I.128-135.1), and on the fate of Themistocles (I.135.2-138).[5] What can we learn from the absence of ἀνάγκη words in these passages?

One probable reason for the absence of ἀνάγκη words is that some of the situations described belong to a past that is all fact, and therefore lacks ascertainable ἀνάγκαι. All the agents are dead and no reliable record of their thoughts and feelings is available to Thucydides. This could explain the absence of ἀνάγκαι from the *archaeology* which, in any event, was composed to give substance to Thucydides' contention that the Peloponnesian War was the 'greatest movement' (κίνησις μεγίστη, I.1.2) yet experienced by the Greek and part of the non-Greek world, and does not therefore involve ἀνάγκαι but facts. For similar reasons, this also explains the *pentekontaeteia*, introduced to give substance to the growth of that Athenian power which, once attained, inspired fear in Sparta and constituted the situation out of which grew the ἀνάγκη to go to war. It also explains the lack of ἀνάγκαι in the three excursuses. In terms of the structure of Book I, these deal only with the ἐγκλήματα—the charges and countercharges—that preceded the actual outbreak of hostilities; they lack any motivating power in terms of the ἀληθεστάτη πρόφασις.[6] The remainder of the narrative in Book I describes the situations out of which ἀνάγκαι develop, but are themselves not said to be subject to any kind of ἀνάγκη. Thus, the account of the Epidamnus affair explains how the relations between Corcyra, Corinth, and Athens developed into the situation from which the ἀνάγκη of an armed conflict between Athens and Corinth arose. The ἀνάγκη itself is expressed in the crescendo of three speeches (one of them in indirect discourse)[7] and the narrative account of the battle off the Sybota Islands (I.49.7). Simi-

---

[2] See above, p. 21 with n.1.

[3] Thuc. I.24-31.2. The only ἀνάγκη in this section occurs in the indirect speech of the Corcyraeans at Corinth at I.28.3.

[4] Ibid. 56-67.4 with p. 27 and n. 18 above.

[5] Two ἀνάγκαι occur in the Themistocles narrative: I.136.2 explains the reason why he sought shelter with Admetus, and at 137.5 he defends his earlier opposition to Xerxes as motivated by ἀνάγκη.

[6] See Thuc. I.126.1: ἐν τούτῳ δὲ ἐπρεσβεύοντο τῷ χρόνῳ πρὸς τοὺς Ἀθηναίους ἐγκλήματα ποιούμενοι, ὅπως σφίσιν ὅτι μεγίστη πρόφασις εἴη τοῦ πολεμεῖν, ἢν μὴ ἐσακούωσιν. The Cylon incident is told in connection with the Spartan demand to drive out the Alcmaeonid ἄγος and Themistocles is brought in, because the Spartans believed him to be implicated with Pausanias.

[7] Thuc. I.28.3, 32.5, 40.3.

larly, the account of the operations against Potidaea provides the backdrop for the First Lacedaemonian Congress,[8] at which the speech of the Corinthians articulates the ἀνάγκη generated by the Athenian hostilities against Corinth, that is, their spread to include the entire Peloponnesian League.[9] At the same time, their speech in part substantiates one of the two elements of the ἀληθεστάτη πρόφασις, namely the fear inspired in the Lacedaemonians by Athenian growth, which will surface again at I.124.2 shortly before the declaration of war. Its counterpart, the ἀνάγκη which the existence of the Athenian Empire contributed to the outbreak of the war, is provided at the same congress by the speech of the Athenians,[10] who universalize the ἀνάγκη by basing it on the common human motivations of fear, prestige, and self-interest.

No rigid rules can be applied to any aspect of Thucydides' sophisticated art, yet it seems true that his general tendency in Book I is to employ narrative to describe how particular incidents, themselves not determined by any ἀνάγκαι, give rise to irreversible situations, the ἀνάγκαι inherent in which are brought out in speeches put into the mouths of participating agents. Narrative relates the growth of Athenian power in the *pentekontaeteia* and the fear it instilled in Sparta, but the inevitability of war engendered by these two factors is reserved to speeches to explain.

Before we now pursue the question of determinism as shown in Thucydides' use of ἀνάγκη in the rest of his History, two observations on the role of ἀνάγκη must be made. The first is that, although the expression ἀληθεστάτη πρόφασις appears once again at the beginning of the description of the Sicilian Expedition (VI.6.1),[11] it is related to ἀνάγκη only at I.23.6, where it states a thesis whose demonstration is completed with the end of Book I. For reasons we shall try to probe later, no other ἀνάγκη in Thucydides receives such an elaborate proof.

The second observation is that in trying to gauge the significance Thucydides attaches to ἀνάγκη as a formative factor in human history, we find that not all the ἀνάγκαι he mentions are of equal relevance to our goal. Our main concern will obviously be with the ἀνάγκαι that arise from a concatenation of circumstances.[12] Those ἀνάγκαι which describe minimum requirements,[13] the

---

[8] On this point, see Cogan (above, Ch. I n. 5) 135.

[9] Thuc. I.68-71, esp. 70.2 and 71.3.

[10] Ibid. 73-78, esp. 75.3, 76.1, and 77.4.

[11] For an interesting but eccentric interpretation of this recurrence, see Rawlings (above, n. 1) 67-70.

[12] See above, p. 15.

[13] See above, p. 10.

constraints a speaker feels in responding to a point made by an earlier speaker,[14] military services performed under constraint,[15] or ἀνάγκαι manipulated to obtain military or diplomatic results[16] are of only limited interest to us here. And even among the ἀνάγκαι arising from situations, not all are of equal weight. For example, Thucydides' descriptions of Themistocles as compelled to seek shelter with Admetus when he was hunted and had nowhere else to go (I.136.2), and as explaining in his letter to Artaxerxes that he had no choice but (ἀνάγκη) to defend himself when Xerxes attacked Greece (I.137.4), are self-contained in that situations and ἀνάγκαι arising from them are limited to one individual and have no bearing on the rest of Thucydides' account. Similarly self-contained is the situation that compelled the Athenians, under pressure of coping with the revolt of Potidaea and the support for it expected from Corinth, to conclude an alliance with Perdiccas and withdraw their troops from Macedonia (I.61.3: ξυμμαχίαν ἀναγκαίαν).

Of greater importance for understanding Thucydides' view of historical ἀνάγκη are some passages that carry on the theme of Book I, explaining the necessity of going to war in a specific situation. For example, against the background of discontent caused among the Athenians by the repeated incursions of the Peloponnesians, the crowded living conditions in the city, and the effects of the plague, Pericles encourages his fellow citizens in his last speech: "When people who are, by and large, well off have a choice in the matter, it is sheer madness to engage in war. But if it should become necessary either to yield and submit at once without resisting to a neighbor or to risk action for one's survival, the person who shuns the risk deserves censure more than he who stands his ground."[17] Toward the end of the speech he urges them to bear god-sent afflictions as a matter of necessity (ἀναγκαίως) and to meet with courage those inflicted by the enemy.[18] Here a war situation is taken for granted as the basis from which a statesman develops a code of conduct for his people: the first necessity is the choice posed by a situation already developed whether to go to war or not; the second is to resign oneself to the unpleasant situations war inevitably brings in its train and which man cannot control. A parallel situation in Sicily is later handled in a similar way, when Hermocrates tries to convince the Sicilians at Gela of the need to take united action against the Athenians.

---

[14] See above, pp. 10-11.

[15] See above, pp. 11-12.

[16] See above, pp. 13-14.

[17] Thuc. II.61.1: καὶ γὰρ οἷς μὲν αἵρεσις γεγένηται τἆλλα εὐτυχοῦσι, πολλὴ ἄνοια πολεμῆσαι· εἰ δ' ἀναγκαῖον ἦν ἢ εἴξαντας εὐθὺς τοῖς πέλας ὑπακοῦσαι ἢ κινδυνεύσαντας περιγενέσθαι, ὁ φυγὼν τὸν κίνδυνον τοῦ ὑποστάντος μεμπτότερος.

[18] Ibid. 64.2: φέρειν δὲ χρὴ τά τε δαιμόνια ἀναγκαίως τά τε ἀπὸ τῶν πολεμίων ἀνδρείως.

ΑΝΑΓΚΗ AND THE HISTORY OF THE WAR 37

Like Pericles, he begins with a general statement: "No one is compelled (to go to war) in ignorance (of what it is) or is inhibited by fear from doing so, if he believes he will gain something by it;"[19] he continues by warning his audience that Athenian actions will indicate more compellingly than his speech what their intentions are;[20] and he finally reminds the Sicilians of the necessary consequences of failure to unite.[21]

While these ἀνάγκαι appear in speeches as exhortations and warnings of undesirable consequences to come, elsewhere we find them in narratives of actual events describing the inevitable consequences of war. Best known is the γνώμη formulated in Thucydides' discussion of *stasis* in Corcyra: individuals as well as states display better judgment in peace and prosperity, because they are not as liable to be forced into situations against their will (ἐς ἀκουσίους ἀνάγκας πίπτειν, III.82.2). The exigencies of war also necessitate the settlement of people in the Pelargikon[22] and the profanation by the Athenians of sacred water at Apollo's temple at Delium,[23] and it is in war, Pleistoanax believes, that leaders are invariably blamed for military misfortunes.[24]

Some ἀνάγκαι created by war have more far-reaching consequences. To allay fears of Athenian naval superiority, Hermocrates points out to the Syracusans that naval expertise is not an eternal possession but that the Athenians have become a maritime power only because the Persians compelled them;[25] similarly, the development of a Sicilian navy is attributed to the necessity (κατ' ἀνάγκην) of meeting the threat from Athens (VIII.2.3). The events following the Persian Wars created conditions in which the Athenians believed themselves constrained to develop their imperial power. From this power Thucydides saw a further net of ἀνάγκαι developing throughout the war, as he has the Athenian Euphemus state at Camarina: "for a tyrant and for an imperial city nothing is unreasonable, if it brings advantage, and nothing is one's own if one cannot rely on it; all things invariably become friendly or hostile as cir-

---

[19] Id. IV.59.2: οὐδεὶς γὰρ οὔτε ἀμαθίᾳ ἀναγκάζεται αὐτὸ δρᾶν, οὔτε φόβῳ, ἢν οἴηταί τι πλέον σχήσειν, ἀποτρέπεται.
[20] Ibid. 60.1: καὶ διαλλακτὰς πολὺ τῶν ἐμῶν λόγων ἀναγκαιοτέρους περὶ τῶνδε Ἀθηναίους νομίσαι...
[21] Ibid. 63.2: φίλοι μὲν ἂν τοῖς ἐχθίστοις, διάφοροι δὲ οἷς οὐ χρὴ κατ' ἀνάγκην γιγνοίμεθα. For a similar sentiment, see the Corcyraeans at I.28.3.
[22] Id. II.17.1: ὑπὸ τῆς παραχρῆμα ἀνάγκης ἐξῳκήθη; 2: ἀλλὰ διὰ τὸν πόλεμον ἡ ἀνάγκη τῆς οἰκήσεως.
[23] Id. IV.98.5: ὕδωρ τε ἐν τῇ ἀνάγκῃ κινῆσαι; 6: παρανομίαν τε ἐπὶ τοῖς μὴ ἀνάγκῃ κακοῖς ὀνομασθῆναι καὶ οὐκ ἐπὶ τοῖς ἀπὸ τῶν ξυμφορῶν τι τολμήσασιν.
[24] Id. V.17.1: πολέμου δὲ καθεστῶτος αἰεὶ ἀνάγκην εἶναι τοὺς προύχοντας ἀπὸ τῶν ξυμφορῶν διαβάλλεσθαι.
[25] Id. VII.21.3: ἀναγκασθέντας ὑπὸ Μήδων ναυτικοὺς γενέσθαι.

cumstances dictate."²⁶ Throughout his work Thucydides never abandons the view that ἀνάγκαι determine the course of imperialism. In fact, if there is any determinism in his work, the dynamics of imperialism manifest it most clearly. From Pericles to Alcibiades to Euphemus, there is no substantive change in the belief articulated by Euphemus at Camarina and expressed by the nameless Athenians at Melos in the form: δυνατὰ δὲ οἱ προύχοντες πράσσουσι καὶ οἱ ἀσθενεῖς ξυγχωροῦσιν—"those who have the upper hand do whatever their capacity lets them and the weak concede" (V.89). This principle is so consistently described as an ἀνάγκη in narrative and speeches alike that we may safely assume it represents Thucydides' own view. This does not mean that all those who, according to Thucydides, recognize the truth of this principle adopt it as the foundation of their policy. Clearly, Pericles, though recognizing it (II.41.4), did not believe, as Alcibiades does, that war is a time for further expansion (I.144.1; II.65.7). Neither does it mean that Thucydides approves of it in the sense that he bases his own moral values on this perception; on the contrary, as we shall see in the following chapter, there are many indications that he does not.²⁷

The ἀνάγκαι Thucydides sees as operating in imperial rule are, in the first place, those that make for its development to start with. They are first articulated by the Athenian ambassadors at Sparta: the hegemony offered by the allies 'compelled' the Athenians, once they had accepted it, to expand their rule under the impact of the universally human motivating powers of fear, prestige, and self-interest.²⁸ The theme is next taken up by Pericles in the Funeral Oration: "(we have) compelled every sea and land to be accessible to our daring"; but he also sees a less elevating aspect to this compulsion: "having at the same time also established in our settlements everywhere everlasting memorials of both good and bad."²⁹ That this ἀνάγκη must run its course is part of Alcibiades' argument in favor of undertaking the Sicilian Expedition: "it is not up to us to determine the limits of our rule, but since we have reached this point it is necessary to hatch plots against some and not to let go of others, because there is

---

[26] Id. VI.85.1: ἀνδρὶ δὲ τυράννῳ ἢ πόλει ἀρχὴν ἐχούσῃ οὐδὲν ἄλογον ὅτι ξυμφέρον οὐδ' οἰκεῖον ὅτι μὴ πιστόν· πρὸς ἕκαστα δὲ δεῖ ἢ ἐχθρὸν ἢ φίλον μετὰ καιροῦ γίγνεσθαι.

[27] A failure to differentiate what Thucydides seems to have regarded as true from what he regarded as desirable is the chief flaw of Rengakos' otherwise perceptive work (above, Ch. III n. 22).

[28] Thuc. I.75.3: ἐξ αὐτοῦ δὲ τοῦ ἔργου κατηναγκάσθημεν τὸ πρῶτον προαγαγεῖν αὐτὴν ἐς τόδε, μάλιστα μὲν ὑπὸ δέους, ἔπειτα καὶ τιμῆς, ὕστερον καὶ ὠφελίας.

[29] Id. II.41.4: ...ἀλλὰ πᾶσαν μὲν θάλασσαν καὶ γῆν ἐσβατὸν τῇ ἡμετέρᾳ τόλμῃ καταναγκάσαντες γενέσθαι, πανταχοῦ δὲ μνημεῖα κακῶν τε κἀγαθῶν ἀίδια ξυγκατοικίσαντες.

the risk that we be ruled ourselves by others, if we do not ourselves rule others."[30] Many of these points surface again in Euphemus' speech at Camarina. His contention, however self-serving, that an alliance of the Sicilian cities with Syracuse will necessarily lead to a Sicilian empire under Syracuse (VI.85.3) echoes the Athenian account at Sparta of the development of the Athenian Empire (I.75.3); his assertion that an imperial power is constrained to be active on many fronts in order not to be subjected to others and to prevent harm from others[31] echoes what Alcibiades said about the limits of imperial power (VI.18.3) and reminds us of Pericles' remark in the Funeral Oration (II.41.1), except that, in a strange perversion of Pericles' statement on the effect of Athenian rule, Euphemus claims that the very existence of Athenian power is beneficial to the Greek world in that it compels those who plot against others[32] to exercise restraint and gives hope to the victims of aggression.[33] Only the estimate of the effect of imperial power has changed; the view of its dynamics as subject to ἀνάγκη has not.

Pericles' statement that imperial expansion has planted memorials of both good and ill takes a more concrete form in a number of passages describing as necessary the kind of treatment to which imperial subjects are exposed and the attitude they adopt toward the ruling power. Here again the earliest observation is found in the Athenians' speech at Sparta. If the leadership against the Persians had remained in Spartan hands, the Spartans would have become "no less obnoxious to the allies and would have been compelled either to rule with an iron hand or jeopardize (their own) rule."[34] Harsh treatment is used to compel recalcitrant allies to pay tribute, supply ships, and provide manpower for the expeditions of the Delian League (I.99.1), and it is even used by an allied state, Acarnania, to coerce Oeniadae into an alliance with Athens (IV.77.2). The Athenians are several times depicted as knowing what they were doing and what

---

[30] Id. VI.18.3: καὶ οὐκ ἔστιν ἡμῖν ταμιεύεσθαι ἐς ὅσον βουλόμεθα ἄρχειν, ἀλλ' ἀνάγκη, ἐπειδήπερ ἐν τῷδε καθέσταμεν, τοῖς μὲν ἐπιβουλεύειν, τοὺς δὲ μὴ ἀνιέναι, διὰ τὸ ἀρχθῆναι ἂν ὑφ' ἑτέρων αὐτοῖς κίνδυνον εἶναι, εἰ μὴ αὐτοὶ ἄλλων ἄρχοιμεν.

[31] Ibid. 87.2: φαμὲν γὰρ ἄρχειν μὲν τῶν ἐκεῖ, ἵνα μὴ ὑπακούωμεν ἄλλου, ἐλευθεροῦν δὲ τὰ ἐνθάδε, ὅπως μὴ ὑπ' αὐτῶν βλαπτώμεθα, πολλὰ δ' ἀναγκάζεσθαι πράσσειν, διότι καὶ πολλὰ φυλασσόμεθα.

[32] Note also that Euphemus perversely speaks of the empire as the target of plots, while Alcibiades had made it the plotter.

[33] Thuc. VI.87.4: ἐν παντὶ γὰρ πᾶς χωρίῳ, καὶ ᾧ μὴ ὑπάρχομεν, ὅ τε οἰόμενος ἀδικήσεσθαι καὶ ὁ ἐπιβουλεύων διὰ τὸ ἑτοίμην ὑπεῖναι ἐλπίδα τῷ μὲν ἀντιτυχεῖν ἐπικουρίας ἀφ' ἡμῶν, τῷ δὲ εἰ ἥξομεν, μὴ ἀδεεῖ εἶναι κινδυνεύειν, ἀμφότεροι ἀναγκάζονται ὁ μὲν ἄκων σωφρονεῖν, ὁ δ' ἀπραγμόνως σῴζεσθαι.

[34] Id. I.76.1: καὶ εἰ τότε ὑπομείναντες διὰ παντὸς ἀπήχθησθε ἐν τῇ ἡγεμονίᾳ, ὥσπερ ἡμεῖς, εὖ ἴσμεν μὴ ἂν ἧσσον ὑμᾶς λυπηροὺς γενομένους τοῖς ξυμμάχοις καὶ ἀναγκασθέντας ἂν ἢ ἄρχειν ἐγκρατῶς ἢ αὐτοὺς κινδυνεύειν.

to expect from the allies in return. At the First Lacedaemonian Congress they are presented as saying that compulsion applied by the stronger is more acceptable to mankind than unjust treatment meted out by an equal in a judicial proceeding.[35] Dislike of the imperial ruler by his subjects is so generally recognized as a given in Thucydides that even Cleon is willing to pardon those allies whose revolt has been due to unwillingness to put up with imperial rule or who have been compelled to revolt by enemies of Athens (III.39.2 and 7). But he also regards rebels who do not fall into these categories as necessarily (ἐξ ἀνάγκης) enemies of Athens forever (III.40.3): their harsh punishment is called for, even if unjustly inflicted, because the recipient of an unnecessary wrong will vent his anger, if he escapes, all the more fiercely upon the perpetrator of the wrong.[36] Against Cleon, Diodotus seems to believe that rebellion was a necessity for the Mytilenaeans and that want drove them into it[37] and he regards severe penalties as useless. In short, Cleon and Diodotus concur that by its very nature an imperial power is at odds with its subjects. This is also the view taken by the Samians at Anaea: in order to escape harsh treatment on falling into Spartan hands, they argue that they were Athenian allies only under constraint.[38] Tight control over subjects is one of the necessities of empire.

The whole weight of imperial ἀνάγκη is articulated in the Melian Dialogue. In a condensed fashion it embodies the ἀνάγκαι weighing upon an empire at war stripped of all pretense. It shows the Athenians seeing themselves constrained not merely to hold on to what they already have, but driven by the fear, prestige, and self-interest which their ambassadors at Sparta had identified as the mainsprings of the early expansion of empire, to reach out without provocation and in time of formal peace with Sparta for a small neutral island[39] that had the misfortune of enjoying a strategically favorable location. Ἀνάγκη sets in at once, but it is an ἀνάγκη manipulated by the imperial power and not determined by a pre-existing situation. When the Melians persist in

---

[35] Ibid. 77.2: βιάζεσθαι γὰρ οἷς ἂν ἐξῇ, δικάζεσθαι οὐδὲν προσδέονται....4: ἀδικούμενοί τε, ὡς ἔοικεν, οἱ ἄνθρωποι μᾶλλον ὀργίζονται ἢ βιαζόμενοι· τὸ μὲν γὰρ ἀπὸ τοῦ ἴσου δοκεῖ πλεονεκτεῖσθαι, τὸ δ' ἀπὸ τοῦ κρείσσονος καταναγκάζεσθαι.

[36] Id. III.40.6: ὁ γὰρ μὴ ξὺν ἀνάγκῃ τι παθὼν χαλεπώτερος διαφυγὼν τοῦ ἀπὸ τῆς ἴσης ἐχθροῦ, with Gomme, *HCT* 2.312 ad loc. On the threat posed by a subject to the ruling power, see also V.91.1 and 99.

[37] Id. III.45.4: ἀλλ' ἡ μὲν πενία ἀνάγκῃ τὴν τόλμαν παρέχουσα, ἡ δ' ἐξουσία ὕβρει τὴν πλεονεξίαν καὶ φρονήματι, αἱ δ' ἄλλαι ξυντυχίαι ὀργῇ τῶν ἀνθρώπων ὡς ἑκάστη τις κατέχεται ὑπ' ἀνηκέστου τινὸς κρείσσονος ἐξάγουσιν ἐς τοὺς κινδύνους.

[38] Ibid. 32.2: ὑπὸ ἀνάγκης. Cf. also the Plataeans' argument to the Spartans at III.58.2 that they had been fighting them only κατ' ἀνάγκην.

[39] On the problematic relations between Athens and Melos, see Andrewes, *HCT* 4.156-58.

maintaining their neutrality, the Athenians with the support of six Chian and two Lesbian ships try to coerce (ἠνάγκαζον) them to join the empire by ravaging their land (V.84). The Athenians' motives, as explained in the Dialogue, are those to which they had attributed the growth of their empire in Book I: fear that an insurrection of their subjects may overthrow them,[40] concern that failure to conquer Melos will impair their prestige among their allies and in the Greek world,[41] and the advantage to the preservation of the empire that possession of Melos will entail.[42] And just as the Athenian ambassadors at Sparta related fear, prestige, and self-interest to the "way humans are" (ἀνθρωπείου τρόπου, I.76.2), their counterparts at Melos appeal to "human calculation" (ἐν τῷ ἀνθρωπείῳ λόγῳ) as acknowledging the validity of arguments from morality only in situations in which the ἀνάγκη of the opposing parties is equal, but not where one party is in a position to exact and the other can only make concessions.[43] The validity of this argument is accepted under duress by the Melians to the extent that they recognize the ἀνάγκη to forego arguments from morality in favor of arguments from advantage—to no avail, as it turns out (V.90). The Athenians' remark on the threat to their power from islanders who have not yet been subjugated and from those who feel provoked by the compulsion of having to live as imperial subjects is reminiscent of earlier remarks on the treatment of subject allies by an imperial power.[44] And finally, with the strongest statement on imperial ἀνάγκη in the whole of Thucydides' work, the

---

[40] Id. V.91.1: οὐ γὰρ οἱ ἄρχοντες ἄλλων, ὥσπερ καὶ Λακεδαιμόνιοι, οὗτοι δεινοὶ τοῖς νικηθεῖσιν..., ἀλλ' ἢν οἱ ὑπήκοοί που τῶν ἀρξάντων αὐτοὶ ἐπιθέμενοι κρατήσωσιν. Cf. 97: δικαιώματι γὰρ οὐδετέρους ἐλλείπειν ἡγοῦνται, κατὰ δύναμιν δὲ τοὺς μὲν περιγίγνεσθαι, ἡμᾶς δὲ φόβῳ οὐκ ἐπιέναι.

[41] Ibid. 95: οὐ γὰρ τοσοῦτον ἡμᾶς βλάπτει ἡ ἔχθρα ὑμῶν ὅσον ἡ φιλία μὲν ἀσθενείας, τὸ δὲ μῖσος δυνάμεως παράδειγμα τοῖς ἀρχομένοις δηλούμενον; cf. 97: ὥστε ἔξω καὶ τοῦ πλεόνων ἄρξαι καὶ τὸ ἀσφαλὲς ἡμῖν διὰ τὸ καταστραφῆναι ἂν παράσχοιτε, ἄλλως τε καὶ νησιῶται ναυκρατόρων καὶ ἀσθενέστεροι ἑτέρων ὄντες εἰ μὴ περιγένοισθε; and 99: οὐ γὰρ νομίζομεν ἡμῖν τούτους δεινοτέρους ὅσοι ἠπειρῶται που ὄντες τῷ ἐλευθέρῳ πολλὴν τὴν διαμέλλησιν τῆς πρὸς ἡμᾶς φυλακῆς ποιήσονται, ἀλλὰ τοὺς νησιώτας τέ που ἀνάρκτους, ὥσπερ ὑμᾶς, καὶ τοὺς ἤδη τῆς ἀρχῆς τῷ ἀναγκαίῳ παροξυνομένους. οὗτοι γὰρ πλεῖστ' ἂν τῷ ἀλογίστῳ ἐπιτρέψαντες σφᾶς τε αὐτοὺς καὶ ἡμᾶς ἐς προὖπτον κίνδυνον καταστήσειαν.

[42] Ibid. 91.2: ὡς δὲ ἐπ' ὠφελίᾳ τε πάρεσμεν τῆς ἡμετέρας ἀρχῆς καὶ ἐπὶ σωτηρίᾳ νῦν τοὺς λόγους ἐροῦμεν τῆς ὑμετέρας πόλεως, ταῦτα δηλώσομεν, βουλόμενοι ἀπόνως μὲν ὑμῶν ἄρξαι, χρησίμως δ' ὑμᾶς ἀμφοτέροις σωθῆναι; cf. also 97 as cited above, n. 41.

[43] Ibid. 89: ἐπισταμένους πρὸς εἰδότας ὅτι δίκαια μὲν ἐν τῷ ἀνθρωπείῳ λόγῳ ἀπὸ τῆς ἴσης ἀνάγκης κρίνεται, δυνατὰ δὲ οἱ προύχοντες πράσσουσι καὶ οἱ ἀσθενεῖς ξυγχωροῦσιν. Cf. above, p. 38.

[44] Ibid. 99: ...ἀλλὰ τοὺς νησιώτας τέ που ἀνάρκτους, ὥσπερ ὑμᾶς, καὶ τοὺς ἤδη τῆς ἀρχῆς τῷ ἀναγκαίῳ παροξυνομένους. Cf. above, nn. 29 and 34.

Athenians brush aside the Melian hope that considerations of kinship will compel the Spartans to come to their aid (V.104): "In the case of the divine it is our opinion and in the case of humans our clear conviction that by a constraint inherent in nature they rule wheresoever they have the power. This is not a law we enacted or first used once enacted: it was a reality already when we took it over and it will exist forever when we shall leave it behind. We are applying it in the knowledge that you and anyone else who has attained as much power as we have would do the same."[45] The drive to dominate others is here described as a necessary outgrowth of a universal order sanctioned by nature, to which all humans certainly (and the gods probably) are subject, whether they like it or not.[46] Power once possessed will of necessity be used; 'nature' explains but does not justify the existence of imperial power, and the Melians will experience the futility of resisting it.

The ἀνάγκαι arising from the state of war and from imperial rule which we have discussed so far can be regarded as 'deterministic' up to a point: they would not have arisen had there been no war and had the Athenians not been handed the hegemony over the allies in the first place. Moreover, they are deterministic in the sense that they have the kind of universality that would probably make Thucydides classify them among the τοιαῦτα καὶ παραπλήσια in which, he asserts (I.22.4), the future will resemble the past. This is presumably one of the reasons why so many of them occur in the narrative parts of his work and do not depend for interpretation on the speeches.[47] Yet it would be wrong to label Thucydides' view of history as 'deterministic' *tout court*. No ἀνάγκη compelled the allies to request that Athens assume the hegemony over them; nothing constrained the Athenians to attack Melos or to develop their empire by the steps outlined in the *pentekontaeteia*. This raises the question how ἀνάγκη situations and non-ἀνάγκη situations are related to one another, or better: the degree to which ἀνάγκη determines in Thucydides the course of the Peloponnesian War as a whole. To answer it, we must begin by trying to discover how ἀνάγκαι enter Thucydides' narrative.

---

[45] Ibid. 105.2: ἡγούμεθα γὰρ τό τε θεῖον δόξῃ τὸ ἀνθρώπειόν τε σαφῶς διὰ παντὸς ὑπὸ φύσεως ἀναγκαίας, οὗ ἂν κρατῇ, ἄρχειν· καὶ ἡμεῖς οὔτε θέντες τὸν νόμον οὔτε κειμένῳ πρῶτον χρησάμενοι, ὄντα δὲ παραλαβόντες καὶ ἐσόμενον ἐς αἰεὶ καταλείψοντες χρώμεθα αὐτῷ, εἰδότες καὶ ὑμᾶς ἂν καὶ ἄλλους ἐν τῇ αὐτῇ δυνάμει ἡμῖν γενομένους δρῶντας ἂν ταὐτό.

[46] de Ste. Croix (above, Ch. I n. 5) 15 with n. 30 has given the *coup de grâce* to the notion that Thucydides is here describing a "might-makes-right" doctrine.

[47] On the consequences of the war, see, e.g., II.17.1-2 (occupation of the Pelargikon), III.82.2 (general conditions of war exacerbated by *stasis*), IV.98.5-6 (desecration of holy water at Delium), VIII.2.3 (development of Sicilian navy, cf. also indirect speech of Hermocrates on Athenian navy at VII.21.3). On consequences of imperialism, see, e.g., I.99.1 (coercion of payments by the allies), IV.77.2 (coercion into joining alliance with Athens).

In order to persuade his readers that his narrative of events is true and accurate, Thucydides has to make 'compelling' even those passages in which he uses no ἀνάγκη words: how does he make them cogent and cohesive? The authority his narrative seems to have for us has recently been attributed to three factors: the intelligence and integrity of his historical method, which he displays at the opening of his work in the *archaeology;* a style that does justice to the complexity of historical events and of human motives; and the 'experiential' or 'participatory' aspect of his work, through which he implicates the reader in his narrative.[48] Unexceptionable though these observations may be, they are too general and imprecise to account for the authority that makes Thucydides' narrative cogent and believable. To the best of my knowledge, there has been no scholarly attempt to investigate this problem comprehensively and systematically, and it is doubtful whether such an attempt could ever be successful.[49] No two events are identical and each is subject to its own logic. Thucydides' narrative shows in its telling that he recognizes the logic of an event, but, though he often relates it to other events, he shrinks from pressing it into a general formula and exploiting it for a theoretical statement.

This does not mean, however, that the structure of a number of individual narratives has not been successfully analyzed for cohesiveness.[50] Of special value among such analyses is Mme de Romilly's examination of the description of the Athenian attempt to invest Syracuse by erecting a wall and the Syracusan counter-efforts under the direction of Gylippus to prevent it (VI.96-VII.8), because she has cast her net wide enough to isolate features that apply to the structure of most Thucydidean narratives and because she provides insights that help us analyze the place of ἀνάγκη in the rest of Thucydides' work.[51] There is no need here to rehearse the techniques through which, as she demonstrates, a given narrative receives its unity and by which it is at the same time integrated into larger units through the repetition of key words and key phrases and through the interlacing of individual episodes with one another. The essential insight gained is that Thucydides' unswerving observance of chronology creates a sense of coherence through the juxtaposition of synchronic events and through

---

[48] W.R. Connor, "Narrative discourse in Thucydides," in *The Greek Historians: Literature and History. Papers presented to A.E. Raubitschek* (Stanford, 1985) 1-17.

[49] For a promising beginning, see C.J. Dewald, *"Taxis." The Organization of Thucydides' "History," Books II-VIII* (diss. Berkeley, 1975).

[50] E.g., Walker (above, Ch. III n. 28); McNeal (above, Ch. III n. 28), esp. 312-18; and the discussion of the Amphipolis narrative as well as some interesting observations on "Parenthesen und Exkurse" by Schneider (above, Ch. I n. 5) 12-26 and 53-66. On the economy of his narrative, see the astute remarks of the late C.W. Macleod, "Form and meaning in the Melian Dialogue," *Historia* 23 (1974) 385-400, esp. 396-97.

[51] J. de Romilly, *Histoire et raison chez Thucydide* (Paris, 1956) Ch. I: "Les procédés du récit," pp. 21-106.

interrelating them with one another and with what has preceded. Moreover, "comme Thucydide élimine tout ce qui est adventice, pour ne retenir ce qui sert à la progression d'une action, et qu'inversement s'attache à cette action sans en négliger aucun élement, il semble que son récit s'érige en démonstration. Les conditions retenues par lui sont, par rapport au résultat, nécessaires et suffisantes. On ne peut rien ôter, rien changer. Et la cohérence même qu'affecte le récit—des premisses aux conclusions—prend un air de nécessité."[52] The "atmosphere of necessity" in the passage analyzed by Mme de Romilly is created without the use of a single ἀνάγκη word; necessity arises only toward the very end of the passage, when the transverse wall of the Syracusans constrains the Athenians to come out and engage in the battle that put an end to their chances of taking Syracuse by land: as Thucydides puts it, "it was necessary (for Nicias and the Athenians) not to ignore the transverse wall that was being built."[53]

There can be little doubt why it is at this point and this point only that Thucydides introduces an ἀνάγκη word into his narrative. Although each step in the account of Nicias' attempt to build a wall and of Gylippus' countermeasures is cogent and compelling, not a single incident was bound to happen the way it did. The steps taken by the Syracusans to prevent Epipolae from falling into enemy hands (VI.96) might have been successful, had the Athenians not been able to outwit them (VI.97). There is nothing inevitable about the Athenians receiving cavalry reinforcements in time to protect them against Syracusan interference with the building of the wall (VI.98). Again, there is no intrinsic reason to compel the Syracusans to build a counterwall or to force the Athenians to take against it the successful measures they did (VI.99-103). The approach (VI.104) and arrival (VII.1) of Gylippus have nothing inevitable about them, and there is nothing inevitable, either, about the initial successes of Gylippus and setbacks for the Athenians (VII.2.2-3.5). Not until measures and countermeasures had converged upon one another to the point at which Nicias and the Athenians recognized that there was no longer a viable alternative to meeting the Syracusans in battle (VII.6.1) does ἀνάγκη set in, marking at the same time the end of Athenian hopes of taking Syracuse by land.

Only rarely does Thucydides use a 'manipulated' ἀνάγκη to develop a situation that creates ἀνάγκαι subsequently explored in speeches.[54] More

---

[52]Ibid. 47-48.

[53]Thuc. VII.6.1: ...ἀναγκαῖον εἶναι σφίσι μὴ περιορᾶν παροικοδομούμενον τὸ τεῖχος.

[54] Such an exception is the narrative of Phormio's strategem at II.83.1 and 3, where he 'compels' a Peloponnesian fleet heading west toward Acarnania to engage in battle against its will, which culminates in his exhortation to his men that their numerical inferiority is compensated by the fact that they are not forced into battle

commonly, ἀνάγκαι punctuate a narrative in much the same way they do in the account of the attempted investment of Syracuse. Thucydides describes a situation, usually without recourse to ἀνάγκη words; out of it certain ἀνάγκαι develop, which may or may not be followed by speeches exploring the ἀνάγκαι from the speakers' particular vantage points. We have seen an example of this in the narrative of the outbreak of the Mytilenaean revolt.[55] No compulsion prompted the Mytilenaeans to revolt before the war, when they failed to enlist Spartan support. Ἀνάγκη entered into their second attempt only in the sense that it made them act sooner than they had intended. When their preparations were reported to Athens and the Athenians failed to persuade them to desist, "the Mytilenaeans were forced to stage their revolt earlier than they had thought" and "were suddenly compelled to go to war unprepared."[56] Ἀνάγκη also marked the end of their revolt: lack of food and of allies combined with the threats of the newly-armed commons constituted a situation in which surrender to Athens was the only viable course of action left to them.[57] Their situation at this point is then exploited by Thucydides to give us, in the speeches of Cleon and Diodotus, two Athenian views of the ἀνάγκαι prompting allied states to revolt which, significantly enough, have nothing to do with the two ἀνάγκαι mentioned in his narrative, sc. the necessity to revolt prematurely and the point at which surrender became necessary.[58]

No ἀνάγκη appears in the eighteen chapters of the narrative of the conflict between Thebes and Plataea, the first open hostile act in the Peloponnesian War.[59] Only at its final stage does ἀνάγκη turn up in the Plataeans' speech to describe their plight to the Spartan commissioners. Earlier, in discussing one of the relevant passages, we pointed out that the Plataeans provide a detailed list of the grounds on which they base their assertion that they speak under constraint, since the cards are stacked against them.[60] The constraint to speak comes in again in their peroration, where they lament it as ἀναγκαῖόν τε καὶ χαλεπώτατον that their speech must come to an end, because with it the risk to their lives approaches (III.59.3). A further constraint under which they claim to be laboring is that, despite their goodwill toward the Spartans, their enmity

---

(καὶ ἅμα οὐκ ἀναγκαζόμενοι) and that fighting in the open sea will avoid the necessity of turning the seabattle into a landbattle (II.89.6 and 8).

[55] See above, pp. 16-17 and 23-24.

[56] Thuc. III.2.1: ἀναγκασθέντες δὲ καὶ ταύτην τὴν ἀπόστασιν πρότερον ἢ διενοοῦντο ποιήσασθαι; 4.2: ἀπαράσκευοι δὲ οἱ Μυτιληναῖοι καὶ ἐξαίφνης ἀναγκασθέντες πολεμεῖν...

[57] Ibid. 27.1: ἀναγκάζονται ξυμβαίνειν πρὸς τοὺς Ἀθηναίους.

[58] For the arguments of Cleon and Diodotus, see above, p. 40.

[59] Thuc. II.2-6, 71-78; III.20-24.

[60] Id. III. 53.3: πανταχόθεν δὲ ἄποροι καθεστῶτες ἀναγκαζόμεθα καὶ ἀσφαλέστερον δοκεῖ εἶναι εἰπόντας τι κινδυνεύειν, as discussed above, p. 16.

toward Thebes has compelled them to go to war (κατ' ἀνάγκην πολεμήσαντας, III.58.2), and this constraint is underlined in the Theban arguments that their attempt to coerce the Plataeans into joining the Boeotian League (προσηναγκάζοντο) only turned them toward the Athenians (III.61.2). Again, we have narrative preparing the situation out of which ἀνάγκαι develop which are detailed in a speech by those most vitally involved. Needless to say, no ἀνάγκη is said to constrain the Spartan verdict against the Plataeans.

One of the most interesting accounts of the workings of ἀνάγκη is contained in the narrative and two speeches recounting the events from Demosthenes' landing at Pylos to the surrender of the Spartan troops on Sphacteria (IV.3-41). A dispute among the Athenian generals whether to proceed to Corcyra (as a waystation to Sicily) or first land at Pylos was resolved by a storm that accidentally (κατὰ τύχην) drove the ships to Pylos (IV.3.1). No ἀνάγκη word marks either the fortification of the place by the Athenian troops or the Spartan countermeasures, which consisted in the occupation of Sphacteria. But that this situation had created the ἀνάγκη of a confrontation is brought out in Demosthenes' exhortation to his troops, in which he emphasizes that action is a more appropriate response to ἀνάγκη than thought.[61] There is no ἀνάγκη in the battle itself,[62] in the defeat of the Spartans, or in their despatch of a peace embassy to Athens. But the Spartans' speech at Athens includes ἀνάγκη twice, each use containing a subtle warning to the Athenians that not any and every condition can be forced on Sparta.[63] More striking ἀνάγκαι surface to explain Cleon's despatch to Pylos, first as an investigator and then as general (IV.27.4), and later in a rather unexpected way to explain the capture of Sphacteria. Their crammed quarters at Pylos compelled (ἀναγκασθέντων, IV.30.2) the Athenian soldiers to take their meals at the extreme end of Sphacteria; this resulted in a fire, inadvertently caused by negligence, which spread over the entire island and stripped it of the brush and shrubbery that had so far protected the Spartans; this in turn made possible the capture of the island and its defenders (IV.31-36). Thucydides' final remark on the Pylos affair, that his contemporaries had not expected the Lacedaemonians to surrender

---

[61] Id. IV.10.1: μηδεὶς ὑμῶν ἐν τῇ τοιᾷδε ἀνάγκῃ ξυνετὸς βουλέσθω δοκεῖν εἶναι, ἐκλογιζόμενος ἅπαν τὸ περιεστὸς ἡμᾶς δεινόν, μᾶλλον ἢ ἀπερισκέπτως εὔελπις ὁμόσε χωρῆσαι τοῖς ἐναντίοις καὶ ἐκ τούτων ἂν περιγενόμενος. ὅσα γὰρ ἐς ἀνάγκην ἀφῖκται ὥσπερ τάδε, λογισμὸν ἥκιστα ἐνδεχόμενα κινδύνου τοῦ ταχίστου προσδεῖται.

[62] Except that at IV.12 Brasidas compelled (ἀναγκάσας) his helmsman to run his ship aground to effect a landing.

[63] At IV.19.2, they express the γνώμη that a lasting peace is not established if a victor forces (κατ' ἀνάγκην) his opponent to swear to unfair conditions; and at IV.20.1 they warn the Athenians that failure to accept their peace offer might force them (ἀνάγκη) to add everlasting personal hatred to the already existing hatred between the communities.

their arms under the pressure of hunger or any other constraint (οὔτε λιμῷ οὔτ' ἀνάγκῃ οὐδεμιᾷ, IV.40.1) sounds like a piece of unconscious irony, considering that the preconditions of the surrender had been created by the ἀνάγκη of the Athenian troops of finding a more convenient place for their meals. Ἀνάγκη has come full circle.

A similar contrapuntal use of ἀνάγκη words in narrative shows how circumstances made Perdiccas give up his alliance with Brasidas and turn instead to the Athenians. After Mende and Scione had joined the Spartans, Brasidas and Perdiccas embarked upon a joint expedition against Arrhabaeus. When after an initial victory they learned that the Illyrians, whom they expected to join them, had actually betrayed them and gone over to Arrhabaeus, both generals decided to retreat. But before a time for departure could mutually be agreed upon, the Macedonian troops ran away in a panic, fearing an Illyrian attack, thus compelling (ἠνάγκασαν) Perdiccas to leave without seeing Brasidas (IV.125.1). Thus, the Spartan troops had to face the Illyrian onslaught alone, which they did successfully; but on reaching Macedonia, they vented their anger against the Macedonians by slaughter and pillage. As a result, "from this point on, Perdiccas began to regard Brasidas as an enemy, and to feel for the future a hatred for the Peloponnesians that was not consonant with the policy he had adopted because of the Athenians. However, he distanced himself from what was necessary to his self-interest and acted to achieve as quickly as possible an accommodation with Athens and to get rid of the Spartans."[64] Curiously enough, Thucydides does not attribute Perdiccas' breach with Brasidas to necessity; necessity involves the Macedonians alone, first in motivating the flight of their troops and then in explaining the policy that necessity should have dictated for Perdiccas.

A curious conjunction of ἀνάγκαι occurs in the narrative of the events following the Peace of Nicias. Almost immediately after citing the text of the treaty, Thucydides describes in general terms its limitations and insecure foundations. He mentions the anti-Spartan movements in the Peloponnese to which it gave rise and then continues: "Moreover, as time went on, the Athenians became suspicious of the Lacedaemonians, because they were not implementing some of the stipulations of the treaty. For six years and ten months they refrained from expeditions into each other's land, but outside it they tried to inflict the greatest possible harm on one another, since the armistice was not firm. At length, however, they felt constrained to break the treaty concluded

---

[64] Thuc. IV.128.5: ἀπὸ τούτου τε πρῶτον Περδίκκας Βρασίδαν τε πολέμιον ἐνόμισε καὶ ἐς τὸ λοιπὸν Πελοποννησίων τῇ μὲν γνώμῃ δι' Ἀθηναίους οὐ ξύνηθες μῖσος εἶχε, τῶν δὲ ἀναγκαίων ξυμφόρων διαναστὰς ἔπρασσεν ὅτῳ τρόπῳ τάχιστα τοῖς μὲν ξυμβήσεται, τῶν δὲ ἀπαλλάξεται.

after ten years of war and to resume open warfare once again."⁶⁵ It is safe to assume that the meaning of 'constrained' (ἀναγκασθέντες) is here the same as it was in the description of the ἀληθεστάτη πρόφασις at I.23.6: a situation arose in which a resumption of open warfare was the only viable alternative for the opposing powers. And just as in Book I the elements constituting the situation out of which the major ἀνάγκη arose were discussed in detail, so here, too, Thucydides proceeds to describe in specific terms the general situation he had outlined at the outset. It is interesting for our purposes that the lack of (a manipulated) ἀνάγκη enters as a contributing factor whenever specific failures to enforce the peace terms come up. At V.35.3 we learn that the Spartans responded to protests against their failure to return Amphipolis to Athenian control and to get their recalcitrant allies in Thrace, Boeotia, and Corinth to accept the peace by saying that they would enforce its terms jointly with the Athenians; they even fixed deadlines for compliance but carefully refrained from doing so in writing.⁶⁶ The situation was exacerbated when in the following year (421/0 B.C.) Spartan ephors hostile to the peace engineered an alliance between Boeotia and Argos, which was subsequently to join the Spartans, so that the Boeotians would not be compelled to conclude an alliance with Athens.⁶⁷ Two manipulated ἀνάγκαι, both negative in character and related entirely in narrative, thus create the situation from which renewed warfare emerges as a new ἀνάγκη.

The ἀνάγκαι posed by the Peace of Nicias lead in a most remarkable way straight over into the issues involved in the despatch of the Sicilian Expedition. Thucydides makes it amply clear that no ἀνάγκη drove the Athenians to accept the alliance with Egesta that triggered the expedition. In fact, he presents Nicias as using ἀνάγκη as an argument to dissuade the Athenians from undertaking an ill-thought-through overseas venture, leaving enemies behind in Greece, "who, first of all, agreed to the treaty under constraint because of their misfortunes and on a less honorable basis than we did, and secondly because we are faced with

---

⁶⁵ Id. V.25.2-3: καὶ ἅμα καὶ τοῖς Ἀθηναίοις οἱ Λακεδαιμόνιοι προϊόντος τοῦ χρόνου ὕποπτοι ἐγένοντο ἔστιν ἐν οἷς οὐ ποιοῦντες ἐκ τῶν ξυγκειμένων ἃ εἴρητο. καὶ ἐπὶ ἓξ ἔτη μὲν καὶ δέκα μῆνας ἀπέσχοντο μὴ ἐπὶ τὴν ἑκατέρων γῆν στρατεῦσαι, ἔξωθεν δὲ μετ' ἀνοκωχῆς οὐ βεβαίου ἔβλαπτον ἀλλήλους τὰ μάλιστα· ἔπειτα μέντοι καὶ ἀναγκασθέντες λῦσαι τὰς μετὰ τὰ δέκα ἔτη σπονδὰς αὖθις ἐς πόλεμον φανερὸν κατέστησαν.

⁶⁶ Ibid. 35.3: λέγοντες αἰεὶ ὡς μετ' Ἀθηναίων τούτους, ἢν μὴ 'θέλωσι, κοινῇ ἀναγκάσουσιν· χρόνους τε προύθεντο ἄνευ ξυγγραφῆς ἐν οἷς χρῆν τοὺς μὴ ἐσιόντας ἀμφοτέροις πολεμίους εἶναι. For ἀνάγκη as the enforcer of the provisions of the peace, cf. also V.42.2.

⁶⁷ Ibid. 36.1 οὕτω γὰρ ἥκιστ' ἂν ἀναγκασθῆναι Βοιωτοὺς ἐς τὰς Ἀττικὰς σπονδὰς ἐσελθεῖν.

many issues left unresolved in that treaty."⁶⁸ However, his argument is overridden by the imperial necessity to which Alcibiades appeals⁶⁹ and which is the intellectual justification for the passionate desire animating the Athenian people to embark on the enterprise (VI.24.3-4); the fact that the same argument for the expedition is repeated later by Euphemus at Camarina⁷⁰ suggests that Thucydides himself regarded imperialism as the driving force that activated the ἀνάγκη arising from the weakness of the Peace of Nicias.

The decision to sail provides the general setting for the ἀνάγκαι that are its logical consequences and which are, therefore, predetermined by it. The majority belongs to the 'manipulated' kind which is invariably part of any discussion of military logistics.⁷¹ The landing of the Athenians on Sicily brought initially more ἀνάγκαι upon the Syracusans than upon themselves. The only ἀνάγκη under which the Athenians labored is identified by Nicias as fighting away from home and with more limited means than their opponents (VI.68.4); but the Syracusans lost the first battle, because they were taken by surprise and were thus compelled to defend themselves sooner than they were prepared for (VI.69.1).⁷² Even the ἀνάγκαι brought about by Alcibiades' defection contain little of interest. Alcibiades disingenuously defends himself at Sparta by attributing his past service to Athens to the 'necessity' in a democracy to conform to the popular ethos (VI.89.4) and by blaming his exile on those who 'compelled' their friends to become their enemies (VI.92.3), his advice to the Spartans includes the despatch of a Spartan officer to Sicily to organize Sicilian manpower and compel recalcitrants to join the Sicilian forces.⁷³ But no ἀνάγκη either compels Alcibiades to give this advice or the Spartans to adopt it. 'Ανάγκη appears only to give a self-serving explanation of Alcibiades' de-

---

⁶⁸ Id. VI.10.2: οἷς πρῶτον μὲν διὰ ξυμφορῶν ἡ ξύμβασις καὶ ἐκ τοῦ αἰσχίονος ἢ ἡμῖν κατ' ἀνάγκην ἐγένετο, ἔπειτα ἐν αὐτῇ ταύτῃ πολλὰ τὰ ἀμφισβητούμενα ἔχομεν.

⁶⁹ Ibid. 18.3, as quoted above, pp. 38-39 with n. 30.

⁷⁰ Ibid. 87, as discussed above, p. 39 with nn. 31 and 32.

⁷¹ For example, at VI.22.1 Nicias calls for the compulsory service into which bakers are to be pressed; at VI.44.1 one hundred vessels are mentioned as commandeered to accompany the merchantmen; and at VI.24.1 Thucydides describes Nicias' advice given in the light of the apprehension εἰ ἀναγκάζοιτο στρατεύεσθαι. Cf. also Athenagoras' remark on the ἀναγκαία παρασκευή of the Athenians at VI.37.2.

⁷² From this follows Hermocrates' proposal for the reform of the Syracusan army, which includes compulsory training for the new hoplite force (VI.72.4), and also Athens' quest for new allies (VI.88.5), which includes Euphemus' argument at Camarina that an alliance of Sicilian cities with Syracuse would necessarily lead to Syracusan rule over Sicily (VI.85.3).

⁷³ This advice is implemented at VII.18.4 by also coercing other Peloponnesian states to join the Sicilian contingent.

fection and to indicate how the Spartan forces in Sicily were to be constituted. No ἀνάγκη demands their presence on the island, just as none—other than imperial ambition—demanded the presence of the Athenians.

An interesting change sets in with Nicias' realization that he must not (ἀναγκαῖον) ignore the transverse wall built against his by the Syracusans, a perception which, as we noted,[74] marks the reverse in the Athenians' fortunes. A long chain of ἀνάγκαι now leads to and follows the defeat of the Athenian forces. All arise from the original decision to undertake the campaign or describe particular military or logistic incidents. They may well be interpreted as a literary device aimed at driving home the relentlessness of the *débâcle*. At VII.57 we get a long list of allies fighting on the Athenian side and constrained by ἀνάγκαι of various kinds.[75] The litany of woes begins with Nicias' letter to the Athenians written after the defeat at Epipolae. He complains that the Athenians are now compelled to use all their ships for the blockade of Syracuse (VII.13.1); that the mercenaries who have been pressed into naval service are deserting (VII.13.2); and that, due to the inability of local allies, the Athenians are constrained to supply both crews and their replacements from their own men (VII.14.2). He draws temporary comfort from his belief that the Syracusans, depending on hired mercenaries as they do, may be worse off than the Athenian citizen soldiers who fight because they have no alternative (δι' ἀνάγκης, VII.48.5). But it does not take long before it is clear that the Syracusans hold the trump cards. Realizing that the Athenians have missed their chance to take the initiative, the Syracusans plan to compel them to fight a sea battle at a spot where the odds would be in their own favor (VII.51.1). And compel the Athenians they do. To prepare for the battle in the Great Harbor, the Athenians compel all able-bodied personnel to man the ships and to take whatever emergency measures they can (VII.60.3-4). In his address to his troops, Nicias says that they will be compelled to fight a land battle from their ships (VII.62.2 and 4), and in the battle itself everything goes out of control: ships ram and are rammed at the same time by other ships, two or more ships cannot help (κατ' ἀνάγκην) getting entangled (VII.70.6), and on both sides the generals reprimand the crews of their ships that unnecessarily back water (VII.70.8).

After the defeat, the only comfort Nicias can offer his demoralized troops for what lies ahead is that they should regard as their own country any spot at which they might be compelled to fight (VII.77.5), and that it is necessary for them to be brave (VII.77.7). The time for strategy and control of any kind is long gone; only when compelled to do so must they even attempt to fight (VII.81.3). The final ἀνάγκη overtakes Nicias' troops as they try to cross the Assinarus River: "forced to march huddled together, they fell and trampled each

---

[74] See VII.6.1 with pp. 43-44 above.

[75] For details, see p. 12 above.

other; some were killed at once by the spears and baggage while others got entangled and were beaten down by the stream."[76] No similar ἀνάγκαι attend the Syracusans or their Spartan allies.

The ἀνάγκαι in Book VIII further contribute to drawing a picture of the Athenians as buffeted about by circumstances over which they have at best but minimal control. After Sicily the number of men available for manning their ships is so low that Leon and Diomedon have to press hoplites into service (ἀναγκαστούς) as rowers as they sail against Chios (VIII.24.2), and Phrynichus warns his fellow generals that Athens cannot now afford to initiate any offensive action, except in a dire emergency (ἢ πάνυ γε ἀνάγκῃ, VIII.27.3). Chios has constrained her citizens to accept an oligarchical regime (VIII.38.3), but is forced to fight a sea battle to break the siege of the Athenians against them (VIII.61.1). Ἀνάγκαι dominate Athens' relations with Tissaphernes, whose support of the Peloponnesians is determined by the fear that his failure to do so will lead to defeat, if they were compelled to engage in a naval battle with the Athenians (VIII.57.1): Alcibiades tries to compel him to side with the Athenians (VIII.88). Manipulated ἀνάγκαι characterize much of the conflict between the troops on Samos and the oligarchical government at home: the former try to coerce (ἀναγκάζοντες) the city to democratic rule, while the Four Hundred direct their efforts at making the army oligarchical (VIII.76.1); the troops are confident that their control of the fleet will enable them to compel subject states to pay tribute to them (VIII.76.4) and to force the Four Hundred to abide by the ancestral laws (VIII.76.6). The only ἀνάγκη manipulated by the oligarchs is their attempt after completion of the stoa at Eetioneia to control the food supply by compelling everyone to store there all local and imported grain (VIII.90.5).

Not until the battle off Euboea toward the end of Book VIII do ἀνάγκαι again arise from a concatenation of circumstances. Their preoccupation with internal problems prevents the Athenians from devoting their attention to the movements of the Peloponnesian fleet until it had reached Oropus. Accordingly, they are compelled (ἀναγκασθέντες) to man their ships in a hurry and with untrained crews (VIII.95.2). Upon arriving off Eretria, they are immediately forced into battle by the Spartans (VIII.95.3), who, with the connivance of the Eretrians, had delayed the embarkation of the Athenians to compel them to sail in complete disorder (VIII.95.4). The Athenian defeat is so complete that, as Thucydides adds, the Spartans could easily have sailed into the Piraeus, if they had been more enterprising, and "either have increased dissension by mooring outside the city, or, if they had stayed to besiege it, they could have compelled the fleet, though hostile to the oligarchy, to come from Ionia to the

---

[76] Thuc. VII.84.3: ἀθρόοι γὰρ ἀναγκαζόμενοι χωρεῖν ἐνέπιπτόν τε ἀλλήλοις καὶ κατεπάτουν, περί τε τοῖς δορατίοις καὶ σκεύεσιν οἱ μὲν εὐθὺς διεφθείροντο, οἱ δὲ ἐμπαλασσόμενοι κατέρρεον.

compelled the fleet, though hostile to the oligarchy, to come from Ionia to the aid of their kinsmen and the city as a whole. Meanwhile, the Hellespont, Ionia, the islands, everything up to Euboea, and, one might say, the entire Athenian Empire would have been theirs."[77] This is the final ἀνάγκη in Thucydides that arises out of a situation.

Was Thucydides a determinist? Although it is possible to regard all ἀνάγκαι passages in Books VII and VIII as necessary consequences of the original decision to accept the alliance with Egesta and sail against Sicily, that decision was itself not determined by any ἀνάγκη. If Thucydides regarded that decision as determined by the nature of imperialism, as the speeches of Alcibiades and Euphemus indicate, there is no evidence that he regarded each step in the denouement as determined by ἀνάγκη to occur as it did and in the sequence in which it did. Short-term ἀνάγκαι, many of them manipulated (and, therefore, not pre-determined) did play their part in individual incidents. That the *débâcle* itself revealed an overarching ἀνάγκη is perhaps intimated in the account of the final fate of the expedition, but though not called an ἀνάγκη, it coheres rationally and has nothing obscure or metaphysical about it.

---

[77] Id. VIII.96.4: καὶ ἦ διέστησαν ἂν ἔτι μᾶλλον τὴν πόλιν ἐφορμοῦντες ἤ, εἰ ἐπολιόρκουν μένοντες, καὶ τὰς ἀπ' Ἰωνίας ναῦς ἠνάγκασαν ἂν καίπερ πολεμίας οὔσας τῇ ὀλιγαρχίᾳ τοῖς σφετέροις οἰκείοις καὶ τῇ ξυμπάσῃ πόλει βοηθῆσαι· καὶ ἐν τούτῳ Ἑλλήσποντός τε ἂν ἦν αὐτοῖς καὶ Ἰωνία καὶ αἱ νῆσοι καὶ τὰ μέχρι Εὐβοίας καὶ ὡς εἰπεῖν ἡ Ἀθηναίων ἀρχὴ πᾶσα.

Ch.V. Ἀνάγκη and Morality

There can be no doubt that Thucydides believed ἀνάγκη to be a force in history in the sense that he recognized the existence of situations that limit the options of the agents involved in them to a single viable course of action. He states this explicitly as his belief (ἡγοῦμαι) in describing the outbreak of the Peloponnesian War as a necessary consequence of the growth of the Athenian power and the fear this inspired in Sparta (I.23.6), and he devotes the rest of Book I to proving this point. The description of other situations pregnant with less momentous ἀνάγκαι, and some of them manipulated by human agents, punctuates his narrative with sufficient frequency to inspire confidence that a belief in ἀνάγκη as a potent factor in history was part of his personal conviction. This does not mean, however, that he sees all situations as shaped by ἀνάγκαι. More often than not, human decisions are free, but once made their consequences are inescapable.

The firmness of this conviction is corroborated by the fact that in several instances Thucydides treats ἀνάγκαι as anchored in the human condition. For example, both at the First Lacedaemonian Congress and again at Melos the Athenians express the belief that a drive to rule others is inherent in man: the fear, prestige, and self-interest that compelled them to develop an empire from the hegemony the allies gave them and not to let it go is part of 'the way men behave'; to rule over others is to do what 'human nature' bids.[1] At Melos, the Athenians claim to be judging and acting within the limits of 'human belief' about the divine: "in the case of the divine it is our opinion and in the case of humans our clear conviction that by a constraint inherent in nature they rule wheresoever they have the power."[2] A corollary of this is also articulated by the

---

[1] Thuc. I.75.3: κατηναγκάσθημεν τὸ πρῶτον προαγαγεῖν αὐτὴν ἐς τόδε, μάλιστα μὲν ὑπὸ δέους, ἔπειτα καὶ τιμῆς, ὕστερον καὶ ὠφελίας; 76.2: οὕτως οὐδ' ἡμεῖς θαυμαστὸν οὐδὲν πεποιήκαμεν οὐδ' ἀπὸ τοῦ ἀνθρωπείου τρόπου, εἰ ἀρχήν τε διδομένην ἐδεξάμεθα καὶ ταύτην μὴ ἀνεῖμεν ὑπὸ τῶν μεγίστων νικηθέντες, τιμῆς καὶ δέους καὶ ὠφελίας; 76.3: χρησάμενοι τῇ ἀνθρωπείᾳ φύσει ὥστε ἑτέρων ἄρχειν.

[2] Id. V.105.1-2: οὐδὲν γὰρ ἔξω τῆς ἀνθρωπείας τῶν μέν ἐς τὸ θεῖον νομίσεως, τῶν δ' ἐς σφᾶς αὐτοὺς βουλήσεως δικαιοῦμεν ἢ πράσσομεν. ἡγούμεθα γὰρ τό τε θεῖον δόξῃ τὸ ἀνθρώπειόν τε σαφῶς διὰ παντὸς ὑπὸ φύσεως ἀναγκαίας, οὗ ἂν κρατῇ, ἄρχειν.

Athenians at Melos: morality depends in 'human calculation' upon an equal constraint on both sides to appeal to it, but not in a situation where the strong can exact and the weak must concede.³ Other ἀνάγκαι follow from human weaknesses: the fact that no 'human device' could cope with the plague and that it struck individuals harder than the physical 'nature of man' could endure made Pericles exhort the Athenians to accept as inevitable what the gods might send.⁴ In a similar view, Nicias tries to encourage his demoralized soldiers by telling them that they are not the first to have done what men are capable of doing and suffered what is bearable in the process; that wherever they are compelled to fight they must believe that the place will be their home; and that they have no choice but to be brave.⁵ Cleon and Diodotus both recognize the fallibility of human nature, yet see different ἀνάγκαι as inhering in it. For Diodotus human nature is a fact that no law can change; it constrains men, when they are in need, to take any risk; once 'human nature' has been aroused, nothing can stop its course.⁶ Cleon, on the other hand, whose views are informed by the conviction that men 'naturally' despise considerate treatment but admire unyielding toughness,⁷ believes that when human fallibility makes men susceptible to be coerced into revolt they can be forgiven, but when this is not the case there can be no compassion for them and they must necessarily be forever enemies.⁸ A view opposite to Cleon's is voiced by the Spartan ambassadors who had come to Athens to negotiate peace and the release of their men on Sphacteria: they bolster their argument that a peace enforced by a victorious power is insecurely founded with the contention that men "naturally are as glad to make concessions

---

³ Ibid. 89: δίκαια μὲν ἐν τῷ ἀνθρωπείῳ λόγῳ ἀπὸ τῆς ἴσης ἀνάγκης κρίνεται, δυνατὰ δὲ οἱ προύχοντες πράσσουσι καὶ οἱ ἀσθενεῖς ξυγχωροῦσιν.

⁴ Id. II.47.4: οὔτε γὰρ ἰατροὶ ἤρκουν...οὔτε ἄλλη ἀνθρωπεία τέχνη οὐδεμία; 50.1: γενόμενον γὰρ κρεῖσσον λόγου τὸ εἶδος τῆς νόσου τά τε ἄλλα χαλεπωτέρως ἢ κατὰ τὴν ἀνθρωπείαν φύσιν προσέπιπτεν ἑκάστῳ; 64.2: φέρειν δὲ χρὴ τά τε δαιμόνια ἀναγκαίως.

⁵ Id. VII.77.4-5: ἦλθον γάρ που καὶ ἄλλοι τινὲς ἤδη ἐφ' ἑτέρους, καὶ ἀνθρώπεια δράσαντες ἀνεκτὰ ἔπαθον.... μὴ ἄλλο τι ἡγησάμενος ἕκαστος ἢ ἐν ᾧ ἂν ἀναγκασθῇ χωρίῳ μάχεσθαι, τοῦτο καὶ πατρίδα καὶ τεῖχος κρατήσας ἕξειν.... 77.7: ἀναγκαῖόν τε ὂν ὑμῖν ἀνδράσιν ἀγαθοῖς γίγνεσθαι.

⁶ Id. III.45.3-4, 7: πεφύκασί τε ἅπαντες καὶ ἰδίᾳ καὶ δημοσίᾳ ἁμαρτάνειν, καὶ οὐκ ἔστι νόμος ὅστις ἀπείρξει τούτου.... ἀλλ' ἡ μὲν πενία ἀνάγκη τὴν τόλμαν παρέχουσα, ἡ δ' ἐξουσία ὕβρει τὴν πλεονεξίαν καὶ φρονήματι...ἐξάγουσιν ἐς τοὺς κινδύνους.... ἁπλῶς τε ἀδύνατον καὶ πολλῆς εὐηθείας, ὅστις οἴεται τῆς ἀνθρωπείας φύσεως ὁρμωμένης προθύμως τι πρᾶξαι ἀποτροπήν τινα ἔχειν ἢ νόμων ἰσχύι ἢ ἄλλῳ τῳ δεινῷ.

⁷ Ibid. 39.5: πέφυκε γὰρ καὶ ἄλλως ἄνθρωπος τὸ μὲν θεραπεῦον ὑπερφρονεῖν, τὸ δὲ μὴ ὑπεῖκον θαυμάζειν.

⁸ Ibid. 39.7: σκέψασθε εἰ τοῖς τε ἀναγκασθεῖσιν ὑπὸ τῶν πολεμίων καὶ τοῖς ἑκοῦσιν ἀποστᾶσι τὰς αὐτὰς ζημίας προσθήσετε; 40.1: ...ὡς ξυγγνώμην ἁμαρτεῖν ἀνθρωπίνως λήψονται...; 40.3: ἔλεός τε γὰρ πρὸς τοὺς ὁμοίους δίκαιος ἀντιδίδοσθαι, καὶ μὴ πρὸς τοὺς οὔτ' ἀντοικτιοῦντας ἐξ ἀνάγκης τε καθεστῶτας αἰεὶ πολεμίους.

to those who have voluntarily surrendered to them as they are to persist even against their better judgment when faced with excessive pride."⁹ It would be foolish to raise the question whether Cleon's statement or the Spartans' represents Thucydides' own view of human nature and the kind of ἀνάγκη it produces, that is, whether men in fact naturally despise considerate treatment and admire toughness, or whether, on the contrary, voluntary surrender is naturally conducive to a compassionate reception. Both propositions have sufficient truth in them to have been attributed by Thucydides to different persons under different circumstances to bolster the arguments from ἀνάγκη which they want to enlist in their cause. This does not invalidate our contention that Thucydides does believe that given situations may contain ἀνάγκαι which prescribe a course for the immediate future: there can be no doubt that he believed, for example, that 'human nature' guarantees that many hardships will befall cities embroiled in civil war, especially in time of war when they are confronted with necessities against their will (III.82). But this perception must caution us against accepting as Thucydides' own view of the human condition every statement about it which he attributes to one of his speakers.

In fact, since he never defines in general terms what factors in a given situation create a necessity, it is difficult to reduce what Thucydides has to say about ἀνάγκη, either in his own name or through one of his speakers, to a general formula.¹⁰ Even a recurrent theme which is nowhere contradicted, like that of the natural human urge to rule others, never becomes the basis for a general theory of human action. Various ἀνάγκαι are always shown inherent in a particular situation, and they can be ἀνάγκαι only because those involved recognize them as such.

Recognition of ἀνάγκη does not imply approval. Thucydides may well have believed intellectually that "those who have the upper hand do whatever their capacity lets them and the weak concede it" (V.89), but that does not mean he approved of this fact. Again, nowhere does he state any principles by which right actions can be differentiated from wrong. Any opinion we can form on this question must be based on the close scrutiny of his text by modern interpreters.¹¹

This state of affairs has given rise in our time to, broadly speaking, two schools of thought in Thucydidean scholarship, dubbed 'modernist' and 'post-

---

⁹ Id. IV.19.2: νομίζομέν τε τὰς μεγάλας ἔχθρας μάλιστ' ἂν διαλύεσθαι βεβαίως, οὐκ ἢν ἀνταμυνόμενός τις καὶ ἐπικρατήσας τὰ πλείω τοῦ πολέμου κατ' ἀνάγκην ὅρκοις ἐγκαταλαμβάνων μὴ ἀπὸ τοῦ ἴσου ξυμβῇ...; 19.4: πεφύκασί τε τοῖς μέν ἑκουσίως ἐνδοῦσιν ἀνθησσᾶσθαι μεθ' ἡδονῆς, πρὸς δὲ τὰ ὑπεραυχοῦντα καὶ παρὰ γνώμην διακινδυνεύειν.

¹⁰ Cf. J. de Romilly, "L'utilité de l'histoire selon Thucydide," in *Histoire et historiens dans l'antiquité* (= *Entretiens sur l'Antiquité Classique* 4) (Vandœuvres-Genève, 1956) 41-81, esp. 57.

¹¹ For a recent attempt, see Hornblower (above, Ch. II n. 5) 155-190.

modernist.'[12] The former is identified as "the older and more familiar Thucydides, the scientist, the rationalist, the pupil of the Sophists and the Hippocratics who had 'grasped and applied the principle of scientific method with such success that his work constitutes a standard of presentation'";[13] the post-modernist Thucydides, on the other hand, is "a writer of intense and complex emotions," who has "a determination to transmit those emotions to his readers, even if their expression involves the shattering of conventional forms of thought, language, and literature. This Thucydides is a person of intense engagement with the events which he narrates and a writer who utilizes a different kind of irony—one who charges language with feeling and intensity instead of emptying it of emotion and involvement."[14] It is true that the focus of Thucydidean studies has shifted in the last few decades. Scholars are no longer as interested as they used to be in examining Thucydides' intellectual outlook as a hard-nosed exponent of *Realpolitik*,[15] but tend to concentrate on his literary qualities and his artistry to see him as a compassionate observer of the human condition and the forces to which it is exposed.[16] There is, accordingly, a tension between those who regard Thucydides first and foremost as an intellectual who sees in history the affirmation of the rule that in politics self-interest (τὸ ξυμφέρον) matters more than morality (τὸ δίκαιον) and that the stronger therefore lord it over the weak, and those who believe him to be a moralist who views with sorrow and regret how the pursuit of self-interest leads to the eclipse of human values. There has recently been an interesting attempt to resolve this tension on the basis of Hermocrates' exhortation to the Sicilians to unite in the face of Athenian aggression: "That the Athenians should try to aggrandize themselves and to make plans to that end is completely excusable. I have nothing against those who wish to rule but against those who are all too ready to yield. For it is human nature invariably to rule over what gives way but to be wary of attack."[17] This passage is interpreted as containing an incipient principle of

---

[12] Connor (above, Ch. I n. 3). For the post-modernist trend, see also K.J. Dover, "Thucydides 'as history' and 'as literature'," *History and Theory* 22 (1983) 54-63.

[13] Connor (above, n. 12) 289, where the quotation comes from C.N. Cochrane, *Thucydides and the Science of History* (Oxford, 1929) 166.

[14] Ibid. 291.

[15] See, e.g., G.F. Abbott, *Thucydides: A Study in Historical Reality* (London, 1925); Cochrane (above, n. 13); more recently, A.G. Woodhead, *Thucydides on the Nature of Power* (Cambridge, MA, 1970), and Rengakos (above, Ch. III n. 22), who, incidentally, has an excellent survey of Thucydidean scholarship from 1919 to the late 1970s, ibid. 13-22.

[16] See above, Ch. IV n. 1.

[17] Thuc. IV.61.5: καὶ τοὺς μὲν Ἀθηναίους ταῦτα πλεονεκτεῖν τε καὶ προνοεῖσθαι πολλὴ ξυγγνώμη, καὶ οὐ τοῖς ἄρχειν βουλομένοις μέμφομαι, ἀλλὰ τοῖς ὑπακούειν ἑτοιμοτέροις οὖσιν· πέφυκε γὰρ τὸ ἀνθρώπειον διὰ παντὸς ἄρχειν μὲν τοῦ εἴκοντος, φυλάσσεσθαι δὲ τὸ ἐπιόν.

united action by the weaker as a way, equally rooted in human nature, to make the combined strength of the weak surpass and defeat that of the stronger.[18] Neat though this compromise is, there is nothing either in the passage cited or elsewhere in Thucydides to support it: Hermocrates does not describe as 'natural' the striving for unity, but the desire to rule (which, as we have seen, Thucydides frequently describes as inherent in human nature) and to be on one's guard; and it is not Sicilian unity that defeats the Athenians in Sicily but the armed intervention of Syracuse's Peloponnesian allies.

However, our investigation of Thucydides' use of ἀνάγκη has given us a way to reconcile at least in part Thucydides the intellectual with Thucydides the moralist. If, as we hope to have shown, Thucydides the intellectual believes that ἀνάγκαι can and do constrain men to act in certain ways under certain circumstances, the fact that they constrain agents to act in ways they do not desire, foresee, or intend (ἀναγκαίως)[19] should enable us to discover the considerations that ἀνάγκαι frustrate or override. In other words, by trying to discover, wherever Thucydides gives us the required information, how men would have acted had there been no constraint to prevent them from acting freely (ἑκουσίως), we can get a glimpse of the moral values Thucydides' contemporaries regarded as desirable.

This method is subject to certain limitations and pitfalls. In the first place, it can yield valid results only when an alternative course of action involves fairly well-defined moral issues; it cannot be profitably applied where alternatives are morally indifferent. For example, we can learn nothing of moral interest from the ἀνάγκη applied by Phormio to entice the Corinthians into battle (II.83.1 and 3); no moral issues are involved in the constraint upon the Mytilenaeans to start their revolt earlier than planned (III.2.1 and 4.2) and none arise from being faced with a choice of fighting a war or being subjected to an enemy (II.61.1).[20] Second, there is of necessity an element of subjectivity in the judgment of what a moral issue is in a given context, especially since the presence of an ἀνάγκη word often indicates no more than that a given action has been performed against (or without) the assent of the agent (ἀκουσίως) and the context provides no clues for the reconstruction of a positive opposite.[21]

---

[18] W.R. Connor, "Thucydides," in *Ancient Writers: Greece and Rome*, ed. by T.J. Luce (New York, 1982) 267-89, esp. 284-85, and the same author's *Thucydides* (above, Ch. II n. 2) 123-25.

[19] This aspect of ἀνάγκη is ably discussed in an unpublished Harvard dissertation by GailAnn Rickert, Ἑκών *and* Ἄκων *in Early Greek Thought* (1985), Ch. I; see *HSCP* 90 (1986) 255-57.

[20] Note that praise and blame follow the choice made, but only the fact of having to choose is described as ἀναγκαῖον.

[21] For example, it would be foolish to infer from Cleon's statement (III.39.2) that revolts are excusable if they take place ὑπὸ τῶν πολεμίων ἀναγκασθέντες that the morally right thing to do is to revolt on one's own initiative.

CHAPTER V

Accordingly, however exhaustive we shall try to be in our treatment, we can hope only to approximate Thucydides' perception of what was morally desirable in a given situation. And third, notwithstanding the validity of the point just made, some ἀνάγκαι constrain (or should constrain) an agent to do the good or morally right thing to do: for example, when Perdiccas' breach with Brasidas is described as τῶν ἀναγκαίων ξυμφόρων διαναστάς (IV.128.5), the policy he abandoned was one he would have been constrained to follow if his action had been dictated by his real interests, and when the Melians believe that 'kinship and a sense of shame' will compel the Lacedaemonians to come to their aid (V.104), their estimate of what constitutes a moral necessity is right, however unrealistic their estimate of its consequences may be.

With these cautions, we may begin to examine what is presented as morally desirable conduct in relations between states. From the arguments of the Corcyraeans at Corinth, we may infer that arbitration of disputes, not resorting to war, and having congenial states as allies (I.28.2-3) constitutes one set of international desiderata, and the Corinthian speech at Athens adds to this adhering to the terms of a treaty (I.40.3). We may include here also the Melian conviction that kinship ought to be a motive for coming to the aid of a state in an emergency (V.104). The same point emerges as a positive counterpart to the ἀνάγκαι under which Athenian allies joined the Sicilian Expedition: the desirable motives for participating in a war should be that it is morally right to do so and that kinship demands it (VII.57.1, 5, and 6) and that the decision to do so should be taken by autonomous states (VII.57.4). Thucydides nowhere passes an implicit moral judgment on the implications of imperial ἀνάγκαι. But he has Pericles extol the daring which has compelled land and sea to be accessible to the Athenians as having settled everlasting memorials of bad as well as good (II.41.4), and makes Euphemus state that the Athenian presence both compels the putative victim of aggression to feel secure without any effort of his own and imposes on the aggressor a restraint that he does not exercise voluntarily (VI.87.4). Statements by the Athenians both at Sparta (I.76.2-3) and at Melos (V.89) that arguments from justice are eclipsed when one side is stronger than the other suggest that moral considerations should weigh more heavily than considerations of relative strength and weakness.[22] From their statement at I.77.4 we can infer that judicial proceedings, even if they result in injustice, are preferable to violent treatment; that gentle treatment of allies is preferable to harshness can be taken as the point made both by the Athenians at Sparta (I.76.1) and by Alcibiades in justification of the Sicilian Campaign (VI.18.3), namely that they present a threat to imperial rule.

---

[22] The same point is also made in the statement of the Melians at V.90 that they employ an argument from the χρήσιμον because the Athenians want to hear nothing of τὸ δίκαιον, and also in the statement of the Athenians at V.105.2 that both gods and men exploit in their rule whatever control they have.

The most detailed guide to the views of human morality emerging from Thucydides' work, both public and individual, can be derived from his account of *stasis* in Corcyra, which in his opinion perverted human conduct because of the ἀκούσιαι ἀνάγκαι ('involuntary necessities') that war brought in its train.[23] Negatively, Thucydides regrets that partisanship brought in foreigners to interfere in internal matters, and that vindictiveness, atrocity, lust for power arising from greed and personal ambition, and contentiousness prevailed. What he seems to regard as desirable is a situation in which daily needs are satisfied[24] and words retain their normal meanings without being perverted into slogans, so that deliberateness in planning (μέλλησις προμηθής), sobriety (τὸ σῶφρον), and intelligence in all action (πρὸς ἅπαν ξυνετόν) retain their traditional valuations. He wants considerations of kinship to count for more than partisan loyalty; he wants the established laws to be observed, pledges to be sanctioned by divine law, and generosity (γενναιότης) to be accorded in giving one's opponent a hearing. Oaths of reconciliation should be observed, public interests should have priority over private, vengeance should be exacted only to the extent that it is just and in the public interest (μέχρι τοῦ δικαίου καὶ τῇ πόλει ξυμφόρου), verdicts must be just, violence must be shunned, respect for the gods and parents (εὐσέβεια) must be honored, and unsophisticated openness must not be ridiculed (τὸ εὔηθες, οὗ τὸ γενναῖον πλεῖστον μετέχει) (III.83.1). Any further indications of Thucydides' moral convictions merely supplement what we can glean from the chapter on *stasis*. Diodotus' speech permits the inference that laws ought to deter men from doing wrong (III.45.3-4); fairness in judicial proceedings seems to be the norm to which the Plataeans appeal in their speech to the Spartans (III.53.2-4); and the plight of Themistocles suggests that it is preferable to find refuge with a friend than with an enemy (I.136.2).

Finally, there are two ἀνάγκη passages from which we can deduce aspects of Thucydides' beliefs on religious matters. The first of these concerns the settlement of the Pelargikon with evacuees from the countryside of Attica. Despite an oracular injunction that prohibited its settlement, ὅμως ὑπὸ τῆς παραχρῆμα ἀνάγκης ἐξῳκήθη.[25] Although Thucydides attacks the interpretation of the oracle then current, which attributed the disasters befalling Athens to the unlawful occupation of the place, his remark that "the war constituted the necessity of settling it; though the oracle did not name the war, it knew in advance that its habitation would never bode any good,"[26] clearly in-

---

[23] Thuc. III.82.2. For an astute analysis of this section, see N. Loraux, "Thucydide et la sédition dans les mots," *Quaderni di Storia* 23 (1986) 95-134.
[24] Thuc. III.82.2: τὴν εὐπορίαν τοῦ καθ' ἡμέραν cf. the situation at the time of Potidaea's surrender at II.70.1.
[25] Id. II.17.1: "it was settled, nevertheless, under the pressure of the present emergency."
[26] Ibid. 17.2: ἀλλὰ διὰ τὸν πόλεμον ἡ ἀνάγκη τῆς οἰκήσεως, ὃν οὐκ ὀνομάζον τὸ μαντεῖον προῄδει μὴ ἐπ' ἀγαθῷ ποτὲ αὐτὸ κατοικισθησόμενον.

dicates that he regards the inviolability of religious injunctions as desirable, and that, while he may doubt the interpretation of an oracle, he does not reject its basic veracity.[27] The second passage relates to the dispute between the Athenians and Boeotians about the sacred water which the Athenians had used for mundane purposes during their occupation of the Temple of Apollo at Delium. The fact that the Athenians defend themselves by saying that they had disturbed the water not in wanton disregard of its sanctity but prompted by necessity and that, accordingly, their act does not constitute a transgression,[28] shows that they regard as desirable a state of affairs in which religious sanctions such as these are respected.[29]

In taking stock of the moral comments we have isolated, it is wise to begin by considering to what extent Thucydides may himself have shared the convictions expressed. The question is easy to answer in the case of the Pelargikon passage: the fact that Thucydides attributes foreknowledge to the oracle in his own name[30] shows that he deplores the violation of religious taboos. His discussion of the pollution of sacred water at Delium points in the same direction, not merely because a similar issue is involved, but because he devotes two chapters to what is basically an insignificant incident. Of course this indicates nothing about Thucydides' own religious beliefs, but it does provide evidence of his recognition of the important role of religion in the fabric of the state. Further, it is almost certain that Thucydides was personally committed to all the values he describes as having been upset by the Corcyraean revolt. The profound perceptions contained in the *stasis* chapter are not attributed to anyone else and do not cite anyone, but are cast entirely as Thucydides' own observations and could be said to reflect his own shock at the phenomena recorded. We are on less firm ground when we raise the question whether the remaining moral principles we have uncovered were also shared by Thucydides. There is no proof that he believed that treaties should be adhered to, disputes between states settled by arbitration, and war not entered into lightly; he nowhere states that considerations of kinship or of morality should carry more weight than considerations of power or advantage, that judicial proceedings are preferable to violence, or that gentle treatment of subjects is better than harsh. In one sense, his own views on these points matter less than the fact that he attributes them to agents involved in the events he describes. But in another sense, these are such

---

[27] See N. Marinatos, "Thucydides and oracles," *JHS* 101 (1981) 138-40, esp. 139-40; B. Jordan, "Religion in Thucydides," *TAPA* 116 (1986) 119-47, esp. 130-31.

[28] Thuc. IV.98.5-6: ὕδωρ τε ἐν τῇ ἀνάγκῃ κινῆσαι, ἣν οὐκ αὐτοὶ ὕβρει προσθέσθαι, ἀλλ' ἐκείνους προτέρους ἐπὶ τὴν σφετέραν ἐλθόντας ἀμυνόμενοι βιάζεσθαι χρῆσθαι.... καὶ γὰρ τῶν ἀκουσίων ἁμαρτημάτων καταφυγὴν εἶναι τοὺς βωμούς, παρανομίαν τε ἐπὶ τοῖς μὴ ἀνάγκῃ κακοῖς ὀνομασθῆναι καὶ οὐκ ἐπὶ τοῖς ἀπὸ τῶν ξυμφορῶν τι τολμήσασιν.

[29] See Jordan (above, n. 27) 129-30.

[30] See n. 26 above.

ordinary sentiments, so deeply ingrained in the mores of Greek society of Thucydides' time, that it would be surprising if he did not himself subscribe to them.

If this conclusion is right, our examination of the values eclipsed by ἀνάγκη confirms a conclusion reached by many scholars on other grounds: Thucydides' system of moral values shows no perceptible divergence from conventional Greek morality.[31] This is remarkable in light of his original and completely unconventional view of the historical process, including his recognition of ἀνάγκη as a force in human history.[32] Herodotus' intellectual outlook cannot be separated from his moral and religious convictions; but in Thucydides a disjunction of intellectual insight from moral sensibility is clearly discernible. Both strands appear to be equally deeply ingrained, so that a compromise between them is impossible. 'Modernist' and 'post-modernist' have the same Thucydides in common, but each chooses to emphasize only one aspect of a complex personality at the expense of another, and each side believes it has captured the essential quality of the whole.

If Stahl is right in seeing in Thucydides' conception of history a tragic element that has as its object "the tragedy of man himself, of man who turns himself and others into victims of his far-flung plans," it is perhaps less because he is "unaware that the perspective which limits his intellectual capability is restricted, and is therefore blind in the belief that he controls factors whose workings are outside his reach (and his power),"[33] than it is because Thucydides knew that his intellectual insights could not make him impervious to human moral sensibilities: ἀνάγκη will always ride roughshod over human judgments of right and wrong.

---

[31] O. Luschnat, "Thukydides der Historiker," *R.-E.* Suppl. 12 (1971) 1085-1354, esp. 1251; Grant (above, Ch. IV n. 1) 93; Schneider (above, Ch. IV n. 1) 122; Connor (above, Ch. I n. 3) 294; Loraux (above, n. 23) 112-14.

[32] On Thucydides' originality, see especially H. Strasburger, "Die Entdeckung der politischen Geschichte durch Thukydides," *Saeculum* 4 (1954) 395-428, as reprinted in H. Herter (ed.), *Thukydides* (= *Wege der Forschung* 98) (Darmstadt, 1968) 412-76, esp. 442-65.

[33] Stahl (above, Ch. IV n. 1) 157.

Ch. VI. The Use of History

Thucydides expresses the hope that his work will be judged useful by those future readers "who will wish to gain a clear view of the events of the past and, in the future, of the events which, human affairs being what they are, will again be like or very similar to them."[1] That this does not state a circular view of history, which would make history a tool for predicting future events, and that the 'usefulness' Thucydides envisages is cognitive rather than practical or utilitarian can now be taken for granted.[2] It is safe to assume that the 'likeness' and 'similarity' of future events to those of the past are predicated upon the permanence of human factors which time will not change. Thucydides draws up no list of these factors and offers no systematic doctrine of what their interplay produces.[3] He is not a political philosopher but a historian; the factors he sees at play in history are embedded in the narrative he gives of them and in the speeches he reports as filtered through his mind. Thus his history is paradigmatic: particular events are chosen, highlighted, and presented as embodying human features that will remain constant through the ages.[4] No doubt one of the insights to be gleaned from a study of the Peloponnesian War is the fact that human life is subject to ἀνάγκαι which, "human affairs being what they are," will manifest themselves time and again throughout human history. To this extent, and to this extent only, can Thucydides be called a 'determinist'. Only to the extent that ἀνάγκαι inherent in human nature shape the course of events can they be regarded as determinable, and again only to the extent that human conduct is predictable. However, ἀνάγκη is not the only factor operating in human affairs: chance, intelligence, reason, and passion are among the many other factors modern scholars have seen as decisive in shaping the course of history in Thucydides, and a still greater number could be identified. Thus, the study of ἀνάγκη to which we have confined ourselves covers but one small and

---

[1] Thuc. I.22.4: ὅσοι δὲ βουλήσονται τῶν τε γενομένων τὸ σαφὲς σκοπεῖν καὶ τῶν μελλόντων ποτὲ αὖθις κατὰ τὸ ἀνθρώπινον τοιούτων καὶ παραπλησίων ἔσεσθαι, ὠφέλιμα κρίνειν αὐτὰ ἀρκούντως ἕξει. On the meaning of κατὰ τὸ ἀνθρώπινον, see Stahl (above, Ch. IV n. 1) 33-35.

[2] See especially E. Kapp's review of W. Schadewaldt's *Die Geschichtsschreibung des Thukydides* in *Gnomon* 6 (1930) 76-100, esp. 92-94. Cf. also de Romilly (above, Ch. V n. 10) 42-48, and Stahl (above, Ch. IV n. 1) 15-19.

[3] See de Romilly (above, n. 2) 57-66.

[4] See Strasburger (above, Ch. V n. 31) 423.

narrow aspect of the 'human affairs' with which Thucydides is concerned; still, it is sufficiently central to enable us to hope that it has value for an understanding of Thucydides' work as a whole. It is now time to summarize our findings.

The importance Thucydides attributes to ἀνάγκη in human affairs is underscored by the prominent position he gives it at the outset as the ἀληθεστάτη πρόφασις of the outbreak of the Peloponnesian War and by the elaborate proof he gives of this proposition, extending over the whole of Book I. Central to the construction of this proof is the argument of the Athenians at the First Lacedaemonian Congress that fear, prestige, and self-interest compelled them to expand into an empire what had been a hegemony assumed at the request of their allies (I.75.3): in short, what had begun as a voluntary act on the part of the allies (I.96.1) was transformed by universally human motivating factors (I.76.2) into an imperialism which, by engendering fear in the Lacedaemonians, created a situation from which a new ἀνάγκη, the outbreak of war, arose. No other ἀνάγκη in Thucydides is as momentous as the ἀληθεστάτη πρόφασις. There are only a few other architectonic ἀνάγκαι in Thucydides. He states in his own name that Sparta's reluctance to compel adherence to the terms of the Peace of Nicias necessitated the resumption of hostilities (V.25.2-3), and through a number of speeches he shows imperial ἀνάγκαι lurking behind the Sicilian Expedition. As a prelude to the expedition, we get in the Melian Dialogue the strongest statement anywhere of the ἀνάγκαι by which an imperial power finds itself constrained (τῆς ἀρχῆς τῷ ἀναγκαίῳ παροξυνομένους, V.95): fear, prestige, and self-interest push arguments from morality into the background when a weak power is faced with a stronger; a constraint inherent in nature makes gods as well as men assert their power wherever they have control (pp. 40-42 above). The expedition itself, as the speeches of Alcibiades and later of Euphemus show, is an ἀνάγκη arising from the possession of empire (pp. 38-39 above).

These major ἀνάγκαι are supported in each case by a number of minor short-term ἀνάγκαι. The immediate causes (αἰτίαι) of the outbreak of the Peloponnesian War—Corcyra's need to look for new allies, the need of Corinth to regard Athenian acceptance of an alliance with Corcyra as a hostile act, and the inevitability of Athenian intervention in the battle off the Sybota Islands (pp. 26-27)—lead eventually to the conclusion in the Corinthian speech at the Second Lacedaemonian Congress and in Pericles' last speech before the declaration of war that war cannot be avoided (pp. 31-32). The ἀνάγκη to undertake the expedition to Sicily is illuminated by Thucydides' statement that Nicias joined it under duress (VI.24.1) and by a whole series of 'manipulated' ἀνάγκαι describing the enlistment of troops and services in the enterprise (pp. 49-50). Finally, the imperial ἀνάγκαι that drove the Athenians to Sicily result in the numerous ἀνάγκαι which beset them there and thereafter in the Ionian War to indicate the extent to which they had lost control over their destiny (pp. 50-52).

CONCLUSION: THE USE OF HISTORY

The fact that Thucydides' narrative of events is relatively free from ἀνάγκαι shows as clearly as can be done that his recognition of ἀνάγκαι in some situations did not make him a determinist. In the case of such past events as the *archaeology* and the *pentekontaeteia* the absence of ἀνάγκη words can be explained by the consideration that the past, being all fact, has no ascertainable ἀνάγκαι. However, this absence does not prevent narratives of the past from creating situations from which present ἀνάγκαι may develop. In this sense the *pentekontaeteia*, in describing the growth of Athenian power and Spartan fear, sets the stage for the ἀνάγκη of the outbreak of the Peloponnesian War, the Epidamnus affair prepares the encounter of Athens and Corinth, and the account of the revolt of Potidaea provides the background of the First Lacedaemonian Congress (pp. 34-35). Yet the scarcity of ἀνάγκη words in the narrative of current events indicates that such strategic decisions as Sparta's invasions of Attica, the Athenian forays upon the Peloponnese, northwestern Greece, Thrace, etc., or the decision of an ally to revolt, are too erratic or arbitrary in their motivations, too subject to chance, and generally too unpredictable to produce any ἀνάγκαι, except a few short-term 'manipulated' stratagems.

Still, as Mme de Romilly has convincingly demonstrated, Thucydides constructs his narratives in such a way that events follow one another in a logical sequence so 'compelling' that the reader cannot envisage them to have occurred in any other way (pp. 43-44). Yet for Thucydides this kind of inner logic cannot be an ἀνάγκη, since at every step of an action a viable alternative can equally well be envisaged: there was no ἀνάγκη to prevent Demosthenes from occupying Sphacteria at the same time that he occupied Pylos, or to make Gylippus arrive in Sicily when he did. The multiplicity of options open at any single step here precludes the operation of ἀνάγκη.

Nevertheless, some events are marked as crucial or paradigmatic through the use of ἀνάγκη words. The relation between Athens and her allies is illustrated by the ἀνάγκαι manifested in the revolt of Mytilene. No necessity is said to have made the Mytilenaeans revolt from Athens, but events compelled them to revolt earlier than they had intended and a lack of allies and food supplies compelled them to surrender. The degree of ἀνάγκη in their action becomes an issue in Athens in the debate between Cleon and Diodotus on the treatment of revolt by an allied state. Cleon's advocacy of harshness harks back to what the Athenian ambassadors said at Sparta[5] and is predicated on his conviction that the revolt had been a voluntary act: if ἀνάγκη, which he views only as capable of being imposed by an enemy, had prompted the revolt, it could be forgiven; since there was no ἀνάγκη, the revolt must be punished. Diodotus agrees that a revolt prompted by ἀνάγκη deserves greater leniency, but his belief that a physical necessity, in this case want, had driven the Mytilenaeans to revolt leads

---

[5] Thuc. I.76.1: ἀναγκασθέντας ἂν ἢ ἄρχειν ἐγκρατῶς ἢ αὐτοὺς κινδυνεύειν.

him to a conclusion opposed to Cleon's (pp. 40, 45). Thucydides' use of ἀνάγκη helps to make this incident paradigmatic for the problems of an imperial power faced with discontent on the part of its subjects in time of war. Thucydides' treatment of the conquest of Sphacteria shows how a major victory can emerge from a concatenation of circumstances that began accidentally. Chance (τύχη) is credited with Demosthenes' landing on Pylos, that is, the occupation is not part of a planned strategy. The stalemate that developed from Athens' refusal to accept the Spartan peace offer, however, placed Cleon under constraint to accept the command, and was resolved by the constraint on the soldiers to take their meals on the island, leading to a fire that cleared Sphacteria for its eventual capture by the Athenians (pp. 46-47).

Finally, we saw that war itself may constitute the situation from which ἀνάγκαι develop. Only two of these are treated as having general validity. One is Pericles' statement on the circumstances under which war should be undertaken: if a choice between going to war or living subjected to an enemy becomes necessary, war is the preferred option (II.61.1), a statement later echoed by Hermocrates (IV.59.2); the other is the statement made in connection with *stasis* on Corcyra, that war compels men, against their will, to do things they would not do in peace (III.82.2). Other ἀνάγκαι are determined by the peculiar conditions of a particular war. Thus, the Persian Wars compelled the Athenians to take to the sea and the Athenian attack on Sicily necessitated the creation of a Sicilian navy (p. 37); the Peloponnesian War made necessary the habitation of the Pelargikon, and the occupation of Apollo's temple at Delium led to the pollution of sacred water (p. 37).

The awareness of the existence of these and similar ἀνάγκαι that flesh is heir to and that were brought out by the Peloponnesian War is perhaps one of the insights Thucydides hoped future readers would gain from the study of his work. Another may be the conviction that the tendency of ἀνάγκαι to override conventional morality need not—and perhaps should not—inhibit the desire to live a conventional moral life, even if the discrepancy between intellectually perceived reality and moral sensibility cannot be bridged and makes the human condition irremediably tragic.

Bibliography

Abbott, G.F. *Thucydides: A Study in Historical Reality*. London, 1925.

Cochrane, C.N. *Thucydides and the Science of History*. Oxford, 1929.

Cogan, M. *The Human Thing: The Speeches and Principles of Thucydides' History*. Chicago, 1981.

Connor, W.R. "A Post-Modernist Thucydides?" *CJ* 72 (1977) 289-98.

Connor, W.R. "Narrative Discourse in Thucydides." In *The Greek Historians: Literature and History. Papers presented to A.E. Raubitschek.*, pp. 1-17. Stanford, 1985.

Connor, W.R. "Thucydides." In *Ancient Writers: Greece and Rome* I. Ed. by T.J. Luce, pp. 267-89. New York, 1982.

Connor, W.R. *Thucydides*. Princeton, 1984.

Cornford, F.M. *Thucydides Mythistoricus*. London, 1907.

Croiset, A., ed. *Thucydide. Histoire de la guerre du Péloponnèse. Texte grec. Libres I-II*. Paris, 1886.

de Romilly, J. *Histoire et raison chez Thucydide*. Paris, 1956.

de Romilly, J. "L'utilité de l'histoire selon Thucydide." In *Histoire et historiens dans l'antiquité* (= Entretiens sur l'Antiquité Classique 4), pp. 41-81. Vandœuvres-Genève, 1956.

de Romilly, J. "La notion de nécessité dans l'histoire de Thucydide." In *Science et Conscience de la Société. Mélanges en l'honneur de Raymond Aron*. I. Paris, 1971.

de Romilly, J. "Le thème du prestige dans l'œuvre de Thucydide." *Ancient Society* 4 (1973) 39-58.

de Romilly, J. *Thucydide et l'impérialisme athénien*. Paris, 1947. (= *Thucydides and Athenian Imperialism*. 2nd ed. Tr. by P. Thody. Oxford, 1963.

de Romilly, J., ed. and tr. *Thucydide. La guerre du Péloponnèse* I. Paris, 1953.

de Ste. Croix, G.E.M. *The Origins of the Peloponnesian War.* London, 1972.

Deichgräber, K. "Πρόφασις. Eine terminologische Studie." In *Festschrift Max Wellmann zum 70. Geburtstag.* (= Quellen und Studien zur Geschichte der Naturwissenschaften und der Medizin 3), pp. 209-25. Berlin, 1933.

Dewald, C.J. *"Taxis." The Organization of Thucydides' "History". Books II-VIII.* Diss. Berkeley, 1975.

Dover, K.J. "Strata of Composition." In *HCT* 5, pp. 384-444. Oxford, 1981.

Dover, K.J. "Thucydides 'as History' and 'as Literature'." *History and Theory* 22 (1983) 54-63.

Edmunds, L. *Chance and Intelligence in Thucydides.* Cambridge, MA, 1975.

Egermann, F. "Thukydides über die Art seiner Reden und über Darstellung der Kriegsgeschehnisse." *Historia* 21 (1972) 575-602.

Finley, Jr., J.H., ed. *The Complete Writings of Thucydides: The Peloponnesian War.* New York, 1951.

Grant, J.A. "Toward knowing Thucydides." *Phoenix* 78 (1974) 81-94.

Herter, H., ed. *Thukydides* (= Wege der Forschung 98). Darmstadt, 1968.

Hornblower, S. *Thucydides.* London, 1987.

Hunter, V.J. *Thucydides the Artful Reporter.* Toronto, 1973.

Jordan, B. "Religion in Thucydides." *TAPA* 116 (1986) 119-47.

Kapp, E. Review of *Die Geschichtsschreibung des Thukydides,* by W. Schadewaldt. *Gnomon* 6 (1930) 76-100.

Kirkwood, G.M.. "Thucydides' Words for 'Cause'." *AJP* 73 (1952) 37-61.

Loraux, N. "Thucydide et la sédition dans les mots." *Quaderni di Storia* 23 (1986) 95-134.

Luschnat, O. "Thukydides der Historiker." In *R.-E.* Supplementband 12 (1970). Cols. 1085-1354.

Macleod, C.W. "Form and Meaning in the Melian Dialogue." *Historia* 23 (1974) 385-400.

Marinatos, N. "Thucydides and Oracles." *JHS* 101 (1981) 138-40.

McNeal, R.A. "Historical Methods and Thucydides 1.103.1." *Historia* 19 (1970) 306-25.

Parry, A. Logos *and* Ergon *in Thucydides* (Diss. Harvard, 1957). Salem, NH, 1981.

Parry, A. "Thucydides' Historical Perspective." *YCS* 22 (1972) 47-61.

Pearson, L. "*Prophasis* and *Aitia.*" *TAPA* 83 (1952) 205-23.

Pouilloux, J. and F.Salviat, "Thucydide après l'exil et la composition de son Histoire," *Rev. Phil.* 59 (1985) 13-20.

Rawlings III, H.R. *A Semantic Study of Prophasis to 400 B.C.* (= Hermes Einzelschrift 33) Wiesbaden, 1975.

Rawlings III, H.R. *The Structure of Thucydides' History.* Princeton, 1981.

Rengakos, A. *Form und Wandel des Machtdenkens der Athener bei Thukydides.* (= Hermes Einzelschrift 48). Stuttgart, 1984.

Rhodes, P.J. "Thucydides on the Causes of the Peloponnesian War." *Hermes* 115 (1987) 154-65.

Rickert, G.-A. Ἑκών and Ἄκων *in Early Greek Thought.* Diss. Harvard, 1985. In *HSCP* 90 (1986) 255-57.

Rokeah, D. "τὰ δέοντα περὶ τῶν αἰεὶ παρόντων. Speeches in Thucydides: Factual Reporting or Creative Writing?" *Athenaeum* 60 (1982) 386-401.

Schäublin, C. "Wieder einmal πρόφασις." *MH* 28 (1971) 133-44.

Schneider, C. *Information und Absicht bei Thukydides.* (= Hypomnemata 41). Göttingen, 1974.

Schreckenberg, H. *Ananke: Untersuchungen zur Geschichte des Wortgebrauchs* (= Zetemata 36). Munich, 1964.

Schuller, S. "About Thucydides' Use of αἰτία and πρόφασις." *Revue Belge de Philologie* 34 (1956) 971-84.

Smith, C.F., ed. and tr. *Thucydides* I. London and Cambridge, MA, 1928.

Stadter, P.A., ed. *The Speeches in Thucydides.* Chapel Hill, NC, 1973.

Stahl, H.-P. *Thukydides: Die Stellung des Menschen im geschichtlichen Prozess* (= Zetemata 40). Munich, 1966.

Strasburger, H. "Die Entdeckung der politischen Geschichte durch Thukydides." *Sacculum* 4 (1954) 395-428.

Valla, Laurentius, tr. *Thucydides: De Bello Peloponnesiaco.* Venice, 1480?

von Fritz, K. *Die griechische Geschichtsschreibung* I. Berlin, 1967.

Walker, P.K. "The Purpose and Method of 'the Pentekontaetia' in Thucydides, Book I." *CQ* 51, n.s.7 (1957) 27-38.

Wick, T.E. "A Note on Thucydides 1.23.6 and ἡ ἀληθεστάτη πρόφασις." *AC* 44 (1975) 176-83.

Wilson, J. "What Does Thucydides Claim for His Speeches?" *Phoenix* 36 (1982) 95-103.

Woodhead, A.G. *Thucydides on the Nature of Power.* Cambridge, MA, 1970.

Indices

Index Locorum

Aristotle
Politics 1304a4-10   23

Herodotus
I. 8-86.1   21n2
III.85-86   21n3

Thucydides
I.1.2   34
I.2.2   10, 21n1
I.20.3   22n6
I.21   22n7
I.22.1   25nn11,12,13
I.22.2   22 and n4
I.22.4.   22n7, 42, 63n1
I.23.6   1n1, 3, 4 and n5, 15, 19,21, 23, 31, 35, 48, 53
I.24-31.2   34n3
I.28.2-3   58
I.28.3   26n14, 34n3, 34n7, 37n21
I.32.5   26n15, 34n7
I.37.1   10
I.37.3   9
I.40.3   27n16,34n7, 58
I.44.1   27
I.49.7   15, 27n17, 34
I.56-67.4   34n4
I.61.3   15, 27n18, 36
I.67.1   28
I.68-71   35n9
I.70   17
I.70.2   10, 28, 35n9
I.71.3   18, 28n19, 35n9
I.71.4   28
I.72.1   28n20
I.73-78   35n10
I.73.2   11, 29
I.75-76   33
I.75.3   29n21, 35n10, 38n28,39, 53n1, 64
I.76.1   29n23, 35n10, 39n34, 58, 65n5
I.76.2   29n24, 41, 53n1, 64
I.76.2-3   53n1, 58
I.77.2   40n35
I.77.4   18, 35n10, 40n35, 58
I.78   30
I.84.4   17, 30n26
I.88   30n27
I.90.3   10
I.96.1   64
I.99.1   12, 21n1, 39, 42n47
I.107.2   13, 21n1
I.118.2   31n30
I.124.2   31, 35
I.126.1   34n6
I.126.2-127   34
I.128-135.1   34
I.135.2-138   34
I.136.2   16, 32n31, 34n5, 36, 59
I.137.4   16, 32n31, 36
I.137.5   34n5
I.144.1   38
I.144.2-3   32n32
II.2-6   45n59
II.15.2   14
II.17.1   59n25
II.17.1-2   18, 37n22, 42n47

73

INDEX LOCORUM

II.17.2	59n26	IV.10.1	46n61
II.41.1	39	IV.12	46n62
II.41.4	38 and n29, 58	IV.12.1	11
II.47.4	54n4	IV.19.2	13, 46n63, 55n9
II.50.1	54n4		
II.61.1	18, 36n17, 57, 66	IV.19.4	55n9
		IV.20.1	16, 46n63
II.64.2	17, 36n18, 54n4	IV.27.4	16, 46
		IV.30.2	8, 46
II.65.7	38	IV.31-36	46
II.70.1	10, 59n24	IV.40.1	9, 47
II.71-78	45n59	IV.58.5-6	17
II.75.3	3, 11	IV.59.2	18, 37n19, 66
II.83.1 and 3	13, 44n54, 57	IV.60.1	9, 37n20
II.89.6	15	IV.61.5	18, 56n17
II.89.6 and 8	45n54	IV.63.2	26n14, 37n21
III.2.1	16, 23, 45n56, 57	IV.74.3	14
		IV.77.2	13, 39, 42n47
III.2.1-4	17, 23	IV.87.1	9
III.4.2	16, 23, 45n56, 57	IV.87.2	13
		IV.87.2-3	14n6
III.20-24	45n59	IV.98.5-6	37n23, 42n47, 60n28
III.27.1	18, 45n57		
III.32.2	40n38	IV.125.1	47
III.39.2	14, 40, 57n21	IV.128.5	47n64, 58
III.39.5	54n7	V.7.1	13
III.39.7	40, 54n8	V.8.3	10
III.40.1	54n8	V.17.1	18, 37n24
III.40.3	18, 40, 54n8	V.25.2-3	48n65, 64
III.40.6	40n36	V.31.3	3, 13
III.45.3-4	54n6, 59	V.35.3	48 and n66
III.45.4	17, 40n37	V.36.1	14, 48n67
III.45.7	54n6	V.42.2	14n6, 48n66
III.53.2-4	59	V.81.2	12
III.53.3	16, 45n60	V.84	41
III.58.2	40n38, 46	V.84.2	13
III.59.3	11, 45	V.89	18, 38, 41n43, 54n3, 55, 58
III.61.2	14, 46		
III.71.1	14	V.90	10, 41, 58n22
III.82	55	V.91.1	40n36, 41n40
III.82.2	17, 37, 42n47, 59nn23 and 24, 66	V.91.2	41n42
		V.95	41n41, 64
		V.97	41nn40-42
III.83.1	59	V.99	30n25, 40n36, 41nn41 and 44
III.90.3	13		
IV.3-41	46		
IV.3.1	46	V.104	9, 42, 58

INDEX LOCORUM

V.105.1-2	53-54n22	VII.21.3	9, 37n25, 42n47
V.105.2	18, 42n45, 58n22	VII.38.2	11
VI.6.1	35	VII.39.2	12
VI.10.2	15, 49n68	VII.48.5	11, 12, 50
VI.16.1	10	VII.51.1	13, 50
VI.18.3	30n25, 39 and n30, 49n69, 58	VII.57	50
		VII.57.1	12
		VII.57.1, 5, 6	58
VI.22.1	11, 49n71	VII.57.2	12
VI.24.1	11, 49n71, 64	VII.57.4	12, 58
VI.24.3-4	49	VII.57.5	12
VI.37.2	10, 49n71	VII.57.6	12
VI.44.1	11, 49n71	VII.57.7	12
VI.68.4	17, 49	VII.57.11	12
VI.69.1	15, 49	VII.58.3	12
VI.72.4	11, 14n6, 49n72	VII.60.3	11
		VII.60.3-4	50
VI.82.1	10	VII.60.4	15
VI.85.1	38n26	VII.62.2 and 4	50
VI.85.3	30n25, 39, 49n72	VII.69.3	10
		VII.70.6	15, 50
VI.87	49n70	VII.70.8	15, 50
VI.87.2	28n19, 30n25, 39n31	VII.77.4-5	54n5
		VII.77.5	15, 50
VI.87.4	39n33, 58	VII.77.7	17, 50, 54n5
VI.88.5	13, 14n6, 49n72	VII.81.3	10, 50
		VII.82.2	10
VI.89.1	11	VII.84.3	15, 51n76
VI.89.4	49	VIII.2.3	9, 37, 42n47
VI.91.4	13, 14n6	VIII.3.1	12
VI.92.3	49	VIII.24.2	11, 51
VI.96	44	VIII.27.3	51
VI.96-VII.8	43	VIII.38.3	14, 51
VI.97	44	VIII.57.1	51
VI.98	44	VIII.61.1	51
VI.99-103	44	VIII.71.6	14
VI.104	44	VIII.76.1	51
VII.1	44	VIII.76.4	13, 51
VII.2.2-3.5	44	VIII.76.6	14n6, 51
VII.6.1	13, 44 and n53, 50n74	VIII.88	51
		VIII.90.5	51
VII.13.1	15, 50	VIII.95.2	51
VII.13.2	11, 50	VIII.95.3	51
VII.14.2	15, 50	VIII.95.4	51
VII.18.4	13, 14n6, 49n73	VIII.96.4	13, 52n77
		VIII.99.1	8

Greek Index

ἄγος		manipulated	12, 36, 44, 48, 49, 51, 64
of Alcmaeonids	34n6		
αἰτίαι	1, 4, 26, 31, 64	military	11-12, 36, 42, 50
ἀκούσιος	57and n19, 59	of speaker to make a point	10, 36, 45
ἀκρίβεια	17		
ἀληθεστάτη πρόφασις	2, 4, 21, 23, 25, 29, 31, 32, 34, 35, 48	values eclipsed by	56-57, 61, 66
		γενναιότης	59
		γενναῖον, τὸ	59
		γνώμη	37, 46n63
ἀναγκαστός	11, 51	δέοντα, τά	25
ἀνάγκη	51	διαφοραί	32
arising from situations	15, 35, 36, 48, 51, 66	δίκαιον, τό	56, 58-59n22
as ἀληθεστάτη πρόφασις	1, 19, 33, 64	ἐγκλήματα	34
		ἑκούσιος	57 and n19
		ἐπαναγκάζω	3
as immanent in the human condition	17, 30, 53-55, 64	ἐπιμαχία	27
		ἔργον	8n5
		εὔηθες, τό	59
as minimum requirement	10, 21n1, 35	εὐσέβεια	59
		καταναγκάζω	29 with n21, 38nn28 and 29, 40n35, 52n1
general	7 with n 1		
imposed by external factors	8		
imposed by historical events	9	λόγος	9n5
in imperial rule	38, 40, 41, 42, 49, 58, 64	μέλλησις προμηθής	59
		ξεναγοί	3, 11
		ξυμφέρον, τό	12, 56
in Peloponnesian War	42, 64-65	ξύμφορον, τό	59
in Sicilian campaign	15	ξυνετόν	59
in *stasis*	14	πάτριοι νόμοι	14 and n6, 51
in Thucydides	8 and nn, 3 and 4, 19n7, 24, 43, 53-57	προσαναγκάζω	13, 14 with n6, 46
treaty obligations	12	πρόφασις	1n2

σημεῖα	22	τεκμήρια	22
στενοχωρία	8	τύχη	46, 66
σῶφρον, τό	59	χρήσιμον	58n22

General Index

Acanthians	9, 13, 14n6	Boeotians	12, 16, 17, 48, 60
Acarnania	39, 44n54		
Acarnanians	13	Brasidas	9, 10, 11, 13, 14n6, 46n62, 47, 58
Achaea Phthiotis	12		
Admetus	16, 34n5, 36		
Aenia	12		
Aeolians	12	Camarina	30, 37, 38, 39, 49 and n72
Agis	12		
Alcibiades	10, 30, 38, 39 and n32, 49, 51, 52, 58	Catherine of Aragon	23
		cavalry	44
		Chios	14, 51
in Sparta	11, 13, 14n6 49	Clement VII	23
		Cleon	13, 14, 16, 18, 40, 45 and n58, 46, 54, 55, 58n21, 65
Amphipolis	10, 13, 43n50, 48		
Anaea	40		
Apollo	17, 37, 60, 66		
archaeology	21 and n1, 22, 34, 43, 65	Corcyra	17, 26, 27, 34, 46
archers, Acarnanian	15	Corcyraeans	9, 10, 12, 15
Archidamus	7, 30	at Athens	26
Argives	12	at Corinth	26, 34n3, 58
Argos	14, 48	Corinth	26, 27, 34, 35, 36, 48, 64
Aristeus	15, 27n18		
Arrhabaeus	47	Corinthians	12, 13, 15, 27n18, 30, 31, 32 57, 58
Artaxerxes	16, 36		
Assinarus River	15, 50		
Athenagoras	10, 49n71	at Athens	10, 26, 58
Athenian empire	10, 29, 30, 31, 32, 33, 35, 39 and n32, 42, 52, 53	at Sparta	10, 17, 18, 28, 31, 35, 64
		Crawley, Richard	4 with n10, 17
Athenians		Cylonian revolt	34 and n6
at Sparta	28, 35, 38, 39, 40, 41, 58, 64, 65	Cythera	12
		Darius	21
Attica	14, 28, 59, 65	Delian League	12, 39
		Delium	17, 37, 42n47, 60, 66
Boeotia	14, 48		
Boeotian League	14, 46	democracy	14, 49, 51

Demosthenes	8, 10, 11, 13, 46, 65, 66	Herodotus	21
		Hippocratics	56
determinism	33, 35, 38, 42, 52, 63, 64-65	hoplites	11, 14, 49n72, 51
Dexandros	23, 24	human nature	17, 41, 53, 55, 56-57
Diodotus	17, 40, 45 and n58, 54, 59, 65	human reckoning	18, 41, 54
		Icarus	8
Diomedon	11, 51	Illyrians	47
Dorian	12	imperialism	2, 37, 38, 49, 52, 64
Doris	13, 21n1		
Eetioneia	51	Athenian	2 and n4, 30, 42n47
Egesta	48, 52		
Elis	3, 13	Ionia	52
English Reformation	23	Ionian War	64
ephors	14, 48	Ionians	12
Epidamnus	26, 27, 34, 65		
Epipolae	13, 44, 50	kinship	9, 12, 42, 52, 58, 59, 60
Eretria	51		
Eretrians	51	Lacedaemonian Congress	
Euboea	13, 51, 52	First	10, 28, 30, 31, 32, 35, 40, 53, 64
Euphemus	10, 28n19, 30, 37, 38, 39 and n32, 49 and n72, 52, 58		
		Second	30, 31, 64
		Leon	11, 51
fear, prestige, and self-interest	29, 32, 33, 35, 38, 40, 41, 53, 64	Lepreum	3, 13
		Lydia	21
		Macedonia	15, 36, 47
		Macedonians	47
Four Hundred	51	Melian Dialogue	18, 30, 40, 41, 43n50, 64
Funeral Oration	38, 39		
Gela	9, 12, 36	Melians	9, 10, 13, 40, 41, 42, 58 and n22
gods and religion	18, 42, 54, 58-59 n22, 59-60 and n27, 64, 66		
		Melos	18, 38, 40 and n39, 41, 42, 53, 58
Great Harbor			
battle of	50	Mende	47
Gylippus	12, 43, 44, 65	Metapontum	12
Hellespont	52	Methymna	12, 16
Henry VIII	23	Mindarus	8
Hermocrates	9, 10, 11, 14n6, 18, 36, 37, 42n47, 49n72, 57, 66	'modernist'	2, 55-56, 61
		Molossians	16
		Mylae	13
		Mytilenaeans	18, 23, 24, 45, 65

GENERAL INDEX

Mytilene 16
  revolt of 16, 23, 40, 45, 57, 65

narrative
  in Thucydides 34, 38, 42, 43 with nn48 and 50, 44, 45, 46, 47, 48, 63, 65
Naupactus 15
navy
  Athenian 9, 27, 37, 41, 42n47, 66
  Chian 41
  Corcyraean 27
  Corinthian 15, 27
  Ionian 13
  Lesbian 41
  Peloponnesian 45n54, 51
  Sicilian 9, 37, 42n47, 66
necessity 7 and n2
  see also: ἀνάγκη
Nicias 10, 11, 13, 15, 17, 44, 48, 49, 50 and n71, 54
  Peace of 14 and n6, 15, 47, 48, 49, 64

Oeniadae 13, 39
oligarchy
  in Athens 14 and n6, 51-52
  in Chios 14, 51
  in Corcyra 14
  in Megara 14
  in Sicyon 12
oracles 59-60 and n27
Oropus 51

Pausanias 34 and n6
Pelargikon 18, 42n47, 59, 66

Peloponnese 26, 28, 29, 47, 65
Peloponnesian League 2, 28, 30, 31, 35
Peloponnesian War 19, 21, 23, 45, 63, 66
  as κίνησις μεγίστη 34
  First 21n1
  outbreak of 21, 23, 25, 28, 31, 33, 53, 63, 64
Peloponnesians 32, 36, 47, 49n73, 51, 57
pentekontaeteia 21 and n1, 30-31 and n28, 34, 35, 42, 65
Perdiccas 15, 27n18, 36, 47, 58
Pericles 17, 32, 36, 37, 38, 39, 58, 64, 66
Persian Wars 9, 10, 16, 29, 30, 37, 66
Phocians 13, 21n1
Phormio 13, 15, 45n54, 57
Phrynichus 51
Piraeus 51
plague 17, 36, 54
Plataea 45
  siege of 3
Plataeans 11, 14, 16, 24 n38, 45, 46, 59
Pleistoanax 18, 37
'post-modernist' 2 and n3, 33 and n1, 56 and n12, 61
Potidaea 27 and n18, 28, 34, 35
  revolt of 27, 36, 65
  siege of 15
proxenos 23

Pylos	8, 11, 46, 65, 66	*stasis*	42n47, 55, 59
		in Corcyra	17, 37, 59, 66
		in Mytilene	23
Realpolitik	56	Sthenelaidas	30
religion		Sybota Islands	15, 27, 34, 64
see: gods and religion		Syracusans	12, 13, 15, 37, 44, 49 and n72, 50, 51
revolt	58n21		
of allies	40, 45, 65		
Rhodes	12	Syracuse	11, 12, 39, 43, 44, 45, 50
Rhodians	12		
Samians	40	Tenedos	12, 16
Samos	12, 14n6, 51	Thebans	14, 46
Scione	47	Thebes	45, 46
'separatists'	23n8	Themistocles	10, 21n1, 34 and nn5 and 6, 36, 59
Sicels	13, 14n6		
Sicilian empire	39		
Sicilian Expedition	9, 10, 11, 30, 35, 38, 48, 58, 64	and Admetus	16
		and Artaxerxes	16
		Theseus	
Sicilians	13, 36, 37, 39, 49-50 with nn72 and 73, 56-57	synoecism of	14
		Thessalian	12
		thetes	11
		Thirty-Years' Peace	27, 28, 30
Sicily	10, 36, 46, 49 and n72, 50, 51, 52, 57, 64, 66	Thrace	48, 65
		Thucydides	
		on his predecessors	22
		on selecting facts	23
Sicyon		Thurii	12
oligarchy in	12	Timophanes	23
Sicyonians	12	Tissaphernes	51
Sophists	56	trierarchs	11
Spartans		tyranny	37
at Athens	13, 46, 54-55		
speeches		'unitarians'	23n8
in Thucydides	24 and n10, 33, 35, 37, 42, 44, 46, 63		
		Valla, Lorenzo	4 and n9
		Xanthippus	32
Sphacteria	8, 16, 46, 64, 66	Xerxes	34n5, 36
prisoners at	9, 13, 16, 55	Zeus	13

www.ingramcontent.com/pod-product-compliance
Ingram Content Group UK Ltd.
Pitfield, Milton Keynes, MK11 3LW, UK
UKHW041425180426
11947UKWH00007B/293